Cambridge Elements ≡

Elements in Child Development
edited by
Marc H. Bornstein
National Institute of Child Health and Human Development, Bethesda
Institute for Fiscal Studies, London
UNICEF, New York City

TEMPERAMENT AND CHILD DEVELOPMENT IN CONTEXT

Liliana J. Lengua
University of Washington

Maria A. Gartstein
Washington State University

Qing Zhou
University of California, Berkeley

Craig R. Colder
State University of New York at Buffalo

Debrielle T. Jacques
University of Washington

CAMBRIDGE
UNIVERSITY PRESS

Shaftesbury Road, Cambridge CB2 8EA, United Kingdom

One Liberty Plaza, 20th Floor, New York, NY 10006, USA

477 Williamstown Road, Port Melbourne, VIC 3207, Australia

314–321, 3rd Floor, Plot 3, Splendor Forum, Jasola District Centre,
New Delhi – 110025, India

103 Penang Road, #05–06/07, Visioncrest Commercial, Singapore 238467

Cambridge University Press is part of Cambridge University Press & Assessment,
a department of the University of Cambridge.

We share the University's mission to contribute to society through the pursuit of
education, learning and research at the highest international levels of excellence.

www.cambridge.org
Information on this title: www.cambridge.org/9781009521871

DOI: 10.1017/9781009521840

First published 2024

A catalogue record for this publication is available from the British Library.

ISBN 978-1-009-52187-1 Hardback
ISBN 978-1-009-52185-7 Paperback
ISSN 2632-9948 (online)
ISSN 2632-993X (print)

Temperament and Child Development in Context

Elements in Child Development

DOI: 10.1017/9781009521840
First published online: July 2024

Liliana J. Lengua
University of Washington

Maria A. Gartstein
Washington State University

Qing Zhou
University of California, Berkeley

Craig R. Colder
State University of New York at Buffalo

Debrielle T. Jacques
University of Washington

Author for correspondence: Liliana J. Lengua, liliana@uw.edu

Abstract: Children's temperament is a central individual characteristic that has significant implications, directly and indirectly, for their social, emotional, behavioral, cognitive, and health outcomes, through its evocative and moderating effects on other social and contextual influences. Accounting for these contextual influences is critical to articulating the role of temperament in children's development. This Element defines temperament and describes its roots in neurobiological systems as well as its relevance to children's developmental outcomes, with a focus on understanding the influence of temperament in children's social and environmental contexts. It covers key developmental periods, situating the contribution of temperament to children's development in complex and changing processes and contexts from infancy through adolescence. The Element concludes by underscoring the value of integrating contextual, relational, and dynamic systems approaches and pointing to future directions in temperament research and application.

Keywords: temperament, developmental processes, social and environmental context, social-emotional adjustment, developmental outcomes

ISBNs: 9781009521871 (HB), 9781009521857 (PB), 9781009521840 (OC)
ISSNs: 2632-9948 (online), 2632-993X (print)

Contents

1 Introduction

Children's development occurs in the context of reciprocal relationships nested within complex, interacting contexts and systems that include both proximal relationships and broader social and structural influences (see Figure 1). An important part of the bioecological systems model on children's development is the contribution of children themselves to their developmental processes and environments (Bronfenbrenner & Morris, 2007). In this model, person characteristics shape the course of development through their alteration of the direction, exposure to, and strength of other influences. Children's temperament is a central individual characteristic that has significant implications for their social, emotional, behavioral, cognitive and health outcomes, directly and indirectly through its evocative and moderating effects on other influences. Therefore, it is critical to account for these contextual influences in articulating the role of temperament in children's development.

The following sections of this Element define temperament and describe its roots in neurobiological systems as well as its relevance to children's developmental outcomes, with a focus on understanding the influence of temperament within children's contexts. The Element then covers key developmental periods, situating temperament's contribution to children's development in the complex and changing processes and contexts from infancy through adolescence. It articulates how adopting dynamic systems-theoretical approaches can inform future directions in temperament research and application.

2 Definition and Biological Basis of Temperament

The concept of temperament is thousands of years old. It has had a variety of definitions, but it generally refers to inherent individual differences in how individuals respond emotionally to their environment and experiences. In ancient medicine and philosophical perspectives, such as the Indian Ayurveda system of medicine and the Greek and Roman physicians and philosophers, temperament characteristics were thought to be determined by the balance of body fluids or humors. With advances in the understanding of neurobiological systems and functioning, perspectives on temperament have evolved, although temperament continues to be viewed as individual differences in emotional reactivity and regulation, rooted in neurobiological systems. Until the 1950s much of the thinking about temperament concerned adulthood. With Thomas and Chess (1977), attention turned to individual differences in infants' reactions to their environments and regulation of their emotions and behaviors, thus launching research on the role of temperament in children's development.

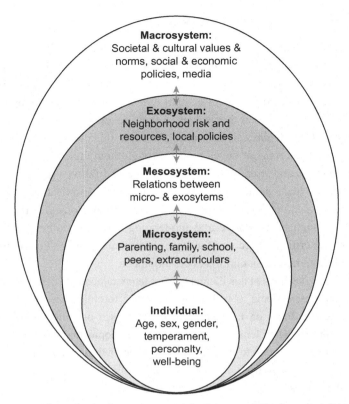

Figure 1 Bioecological systems model of the contribution of children's temperament in interaction and transaction with social and contextual influences and developmental processes.

Since then, research with children has been grounded predominantly in four temperament approaches (Goldsmith et al., 1987). Thomas and Chess (1977) identified individual differences across nine dimensions (activity, regularity, reactivity, adaptability, intensity, mood, distractibility, persistence, and sensory threshold) and introduced the terms "easy," "difficult," and "slow to warm" as child temperament styles. Their work inspired the "goodness-of-fit" model which proposes that the match between child temperament and the environment determines children's developmental outcomes. Buss and Plomin (1975) focused on temperament traits with a genetic basis and employed a gene-by-environment approach, seeking to understand the relative contributions of each, as well as their interactions, to temperamental and behavioral phenotypes. In another approach, Goldsmith considered the impact of predispositions toward experiencing and acting on different types of emotions and the use of observational methods (Goldsmith & Campos, 1982). Rothbart's model of temperament focused on definitions and operationalizations of the characteristic ways in which individuals may respond to situational demands and facets of behaviors, physiological responses, emotions, and attention specific to certain contexts (Rothbart et al., 2003). It also introduced executive attention as a component of temperament that serves as a basis for regulation.

2.1 Definition

Temperament is commonly defined as the physiological basis for individual differences in reactivity and self-regulation, including motivation, affect, activity, attention, and inhibitory control characteristics. These individual differences are genetically based, biologically rooted, present early in life, relatively stable, and shaped by experience (Rothbart, 2011; Rothbart & Bates, 2007). Reactivity refers to responsiveness to changes in external and internal environments. It includes physiological and emotional reactions related to negative and positive affect. Dimensions of negative reactivity include frustration (anger, irritability) and fear (inhibition, withdrawal), which are thought to indicate activity in the behavioral activation system (BAS, frustration reactivity) and behavioral inhibition system (BIS, fear reactivity) as articulated in Gray and McNaughton's (1996, 2000) conception of temperament. Individual differences in frustration reactions generally arise in response to a goal or reward being blocked or removed, or to a perceived hostile intent. Individual differences in fear reactions generally reflect responses to novel or uncertain situations that present a perceived threat of negative consequences. Dimensions of positive reactivity include approach, pleasure, smiling, and laughter, sometimes combined into a dimension of surgency, and are rooted in the BAS that motivates reward sensitivity (Gray & McNaughton, 1996). Conversely, low positive affect is associated with sadness. Self-regulation refers to executive control processes and behaviors that operate to modulate physiological, affective, or behavioral reactivity. Self-regulation includes attention focusing and shifting, cognitive and behavioral inhibitory control, and delay ability in reward contexts, which compose the construct of effortful control and facilitate the regulation of attention, emotions, and behavior to flexibly match the demands of a given situation (Rothbart & Bates, 2007).

Temperament is genetically based, with estimates of genetic contribution in the 0.20 to 0.60 range (e.g., Saudino & Wang, 2012). It is also moderately stable across proximal developmental periods of childhood, with stability estimates typically in the 0.30 to 0.50 range. Estimates of stability are generally robust across potential moderators (Bornstein et al., 2019), although magnitudes depend on measurement method (e.g., parent report, laboratory assessment), children's and mothers' age, parent education, length of time span between measurements, and whether estimates are corrected for unreliability (Bornstein et al., 2017, 2019; Kopala-Sibley et al., 2018; Putnam et al., 2008). Continuity of similar behaviors over time, referred to as homotypic continuity, is readily observed, especially later in childhood and adolescence. However, a great deal of continuity during early childhood is heterotypic, wherein an underlying characteristic is preserved over time, yet its manifestations vary with development. For example, behavioral inhibition presents as distress to novelty early in infancy, and later turns to hesitation to approach novel objects or situations (Putnam et al., 2008). Given estimates of moderate genetic contribution, stability and continuity, it is not surprising that experience and context play considerable roles in shaping the expression of temperament (Rothbart & Bates, 2007). Thus, temperament represents characteristics present early in life that shape and are shaped by family and environmental interactions and result in differential responsiveness to socialization experiences.

2.2 Temperament and Personality

The constructs of temperament and personality are closely related, and the conceptual basis for this relation has been the topic of much investigation and some debate. Some authorities view personality dimensions as encompassing temperament, others consider temperament as representing a developmentally different set of dimensions, and yet others view temperament as the developmental precursor and core of later emerging personality characteristics (see De Pauw, 2016 for overview). The five factor model (FFM) of personality which consists of dimensions of extraversion, agreeableness, conscientiousness, neuroticism, and openness to experience (McCrae & John, 1992) has most commonly been studied in relation to temperament. For example, temperament negative reactivity is closely related to neuroticism, defined as the disposition to experience negative affect, including anger, anxiety, irritability, emotional instability, and depression (Shiner & Caspi, 2012; Tackett et al., 2008). Similarly, effortful control is related to conscientiousness, which refers to a concentrated, reliable, and achievement-oriented attitude in worklike situations with high levels of involvement and perseverance (Eisenberg et al., 2014).

One conceptual model of the association of temperament with FFM articulates a progression from early childhood temperament characteristics to developing FFM characteristics (De Pauw, 2016). Temperament represents a specific set of core, biologically based individual differences in reactivity and regulation characteristics, whereas personality represents a broader set of constructs that may encompass temperament and also includes cognitive and social components that elaborate or are "layered around" core temperament characteristics (e.g., Rothbart, 2011). Starting early in life, individual differences in temperament shape and are shaped by socialization and contextual experiences that contribute to an individual's cognitive and behavioral styles or personality traits. For example, negative reactivity might contribute to challenging interpersonal interactions, which together shape later emerging cognitive styles to be more negatively biased, contributing to neuroticism. Conversely, early effortful control likely facilitates engagement in supported learning experiences that enhance a sense of efficacy and agency, perhaps leading to greater conscientiousness. As a result, early emerging individual differences might shape the manifestation of subsequent personality characteristics in transaction with key relationships, interactions, and socialization experiences. In this Element, we elaborate on the relevant socialization relationships and contexts at different developmental stages from infancy through adolescence and the roles they play in children's social, emotional, and behavioral developmental outcomes.

2.3 Neurobiological Systems Underlying Temperament

Research has identified genetic, neural, and physiological systems that are the basis for temperament. Neurobiological systems most often studied with respect to temperament include left/right frontal activation asymmetry, respiratory sinus arrhythmia, executive function, and hypothalamic–pituitary–adrenocortical (HPA)-axis activity.

2.3.1 Genetic Basis of Temperament

The genetic basis of temperament traits has been theorized and supported empirically across developmental periods. Behavioral genetics studies suggest that 20–60 percent of variability in temperamental reactive (e.g., activity level, sociability, positive and negative affect) and regulatory (e.g., inhibitory control, attentional focusing) traits can be explained by genetic factors (e.g., Saudino & Wang, 2012). In infancy, frustration, fear, and activity have been explained largely by additive genetic effects (combined effects of alleles on a single gene or two or more genes on a phenotype; Goldsmith et al., 1999). Lemery-Chalfant et al. (2008) reported heritability ranging from 68–79 percent for parental reports of effortful control, and a heritability estimate of 83 percent for observer ratings of attentional control in middle childhood. In adolescence and adulthood, strong genetic contributions to harm avoidance, sensation-seeking, and reward dependence have been reported (e.g., Heiman et al., 2003; Heiman et al., 2004).

Studies have also considered associations between behavioral traits and "candidate" genes, typically considering variants of single nucleotide polymorphisms (SNP). Although there was considerable excitement about linking candidate SNPs with temperament variability, the utility of this work has been called into question because of the complexity of the human genome and genome-wide association studies (GWAS) becoming more prominent. For example, the 5-HTTLPR polymorphism in the promoter region of the serotonin transporter gene SLC6A4 has been described as demonstrating consistent and strong links with a large array of temperament tendencies as well as depression (Licht et al., 2011; see Saudino & Wang, 2012 for review). Yet, a meta-analysis of data from large population-based and case-control samples (Ns ranging from 62,138 to 443,264 across subsamples), as well as preregistered analyses examining candidate gene polymorphism main effects and gene-by-environment interactions, indicated that depression candidate genes were no more associated with depression phenotypes than noncandidate genes (Border et al., 2019). More recent research suggests complex genetic interactions with genes critical to fetal neurodevelopment playing a role in the origins of psychopathology, wherein not only do multiple genes have synergistic effects as networks, but a single gene can have multiple effects in terms of psychological symptoms or disorders. For example, pleiotropic (i.e., associated with more than one disorder) loci within genes that show heightened expression in the brain beginning *in utero* and playing prominent roles in neurodevelopmental processes have been implicated in disorders such as major depression (Cross-Disorder Group of the Psychiatric Genomics Consortium, 2019), and should be considered with respect to temperament.

2.3.2 Behavioral Activation and Inhibition Systems

Approach (fight), inhibition (flight), and freeze systems rooted in the sympathetic branch of the autonomic nervous system, as well as parasympathetic and prefrontal cortex (PFC) brain systems, provide much of the biological foundation for temperament, contributing to reactivity and emotion regulation. These systems coordinate different areas of the brain as well as peripheral activity (e.g., of the vagus nerve) as a foundation for motivation, emotion, and behavior. Although some aspects of these systems and the mechanisms behind their coordination remain elusive, a great deal has been learned by relying on neuroimaging techniques.

Work examining the inhibition (flight) system is both theoretical and empirical in nature. Withdrawal motivational responses were theorized to be part of an avoidance system, which has acquired a number of different names, including behavioral inhibition system, fight–flight system (sometimes referred to as fight–flight–freeze system), and threat avoidance system. Regardless of the specific terms used, they share a common focus on responses to signals of punishment and nonreward, that is, the potential for a negative consequence. This responsiveness to punishment and nonreward includes readiness for action (arousal level) and heightened attention to cues of threat or danger. Behavioral inhibition is a tendency of some children to withdraw or react negatively in response to novelty or uncertainty, including people, places, events, and objects (Garcia Coll et al., 1984). Behavioral inhibition is typically experienced together with fear on the emotional level. Thus, the BIS is thought to support fear and avoidance, orient to cues of punishment and nonreward, and to be capable of arresting behavior that serves to achieve approach or reward-related goals (Gray & McNaughton, 1996). Jerome Kagan's work focused on behavioral inhibition, generally defined as hesitancy to approach new or unfamiliar objects or situations (Kagan, 1998). Inhibited children can be described as shy, cautious, fearful, and motorically tense, whereas uninhibited children tend to be social and outgoing (extraverted) in novel situations, and do not show as much motor restraint as inhibited children. Kagan and colleagues viewed these temperament types as reflecting individual differences in underlying biological processes, reporting a number of physiological differences between inhibited and uninhibited youngsters (e.g., Kagan & Fox, 2006). Specifically, Kagan proposed that inhibited and uninhibited temperament types were a function of differences in the reactivity of the limbic system, and the amygdala in particular (Kagan & Snidman, 2004).

Biological models of sensitivity to reward and approach invoke the BAS in their explanations and definitions. This system is responsible for positive emotional experiences including joy, delight, or pleasure in the anticipation of reward and positive outcomes, as well as anger or frustration when reward approach and attainment are blocked, potentially resulting in aggression (Gray & McNaughton, 1996). This appetitive–motivational system motivates approach behavior, including goal-directed actions and risk-taking. The neurobiological foundations for reward approach and threat-sensitive systems are described in the next subsection.

2.3.3 Left/Right Frontal Asymmetry

Well-established models describing neurobiological foundations of the BAS and the fight side of the fight–flight system, as well as the BIS and flight (and/or freeze) aspect, have focused on asymmetrical activation of the frontal cortex and lateralization of approach/avoidance activity (Fox, 1994) using electroencephalogram (EEG) technologies to measure electrical activity. The left and right frontal cortical regions are asymmetrically related to approach and avoidance motivational and emotional tendencies. Greater trait approach and reward sensitivity are reflected in relatively stronger left-frontal activation, whereas a greater tendency toward inhibition and withdrawal is reflected in dominant right-frontal activation (e.g., Calkins et al., 1996; Gartstein, 2019; Hane et al., 2008). Behavioral inhibition system activation involves the amygdala, basal ganglia, and hypothalamus, all parts of the limbic system, as well as the right dorsolateral PFC and the right temporal region, associated with right-hemisphere dominance discerned via an asymmetric pattern of frontal EEG activity (Kagan & Snidman, 2004; Sutton & Davidson, 1997). The BAS recruits the corticolimbic–striatal–thalamic network and relies on dopamine pathways from the ventral tegmental area to the subcortical and frontal cortical regions, favoring left-frontal activation. Dopamine pathways involve a variety of critical functions, such as movement and neuroendocrine control, as well as reward motivation and executive functions (Coan & Allen, 2004; Depue & Collins, 1999). Although EEG asymmetry measures electrical activity at the cortex, the pattern of lateralization – right- versus left-frontal dominance – is reflective of underlying brain activity that involves limbic structures critical to emotional processes (e.g., amygdala). The BIS and BAS are thought to work in tandem (Fox, 1994), and this mutual regulation was recently examined across development, indicating coordinated action across the two hemispheres and links between developmental shifts in brain activity and temperament (Gartstein et al., 2020).

2.3.4 Respiratory Sinus Arrhythmia

Respiratory sinus arrhythmia (RSA) is a widely used cardiac indicator of parasympathetic activation that has been linked to reactivity and emotion regulation in childhood (Beauchaine, 2015). Variability in heart rate in response to respiration is mediated primarily by activity of the vagus nerve. Vagal influence diminishes during inhalation, resulting in heart rate acceleration, and increases during exhalation, causing heart rate deceleration. The characteristic respiratory rhythm of RSA provides a noninvasive measure of cardiac vagal tone and peripheral regulation (Porges, 1997). Both trait-like or baseline RSA and changes in RSA in response to challenges are related to temperament. In infants, higher baseline RSA occurs with lower negativity and the need for less calming from parents (Huffman et al., 1998). In older children, high RSA is related to better social skills, more efficient mental processes, and better behavioral regulation (Doussard-Roosevelt et al., 1997). Changes in cardiac vagal tone in response to challenges reflect the vagal brake through which rapid inhibition and disinhibition of vagal tone to the heart (i.e., via the sinoatrial node, which is the heart's pacemaker) can rapidly mobilize or calm an individual. Infant research has shown the importance of the vagal brake in the regulation of social and attentional behaviors that require an awareness of the environment and the ability to engage or disengage (Graziano & Derefinko, 2013). Overall, trait-like RSA reflects reactive tendencies, whereas decreases in RSA during challenging encounters are markers of attention-based regulation of emotion and behavior (Porges, 1997, 2011).

2.3.5 Executive Control

Effortful control is conceptualized as the executive-based core of self-regulation, and there is considerable overlap in the conceptualization and operationalization of effortful control and executive function. Effortful control plays a role in top-down regulation of cognition, emotion, and behavior, with executive attention serving as a core mechanism (Tiego et al., 2020). Executive functioning includes attention regulation, inhibitory control, and cognitive flexibility, components that overlap with effortful control, but executive functioning also includes higher-order functions such as planning, decision-making, and problem-solving, that is, complex cognitive strategies that can arise from the application of basic executive-control processes (Nigg, 2017). Thus, conceptually, effortful control represents the attention regulation and inhibitory core of executive functions that emerge in early childhood and serve as the basis for more complex cognitive and behavioral self-regulation capacities that develop later. Studies that simultaneously examine effortful control and executive function identify substantial overlap, including evidence of an underlying common factor (Kälin & Roebers, 2021; Lin et al., 2019; Schmidt et al., 2022; Tiego et al., 2020) composed of attentional and inhibitory control (Kim-Spoon et al., 2019) and shared genetic influence explained by executive attention (Rea-Sandin et al., 2023).

Attention processes present in infancy contribute to executive-control development (Marcovitch et al., 2016). This executive attention-based regulatory capacity emerges in early childhood, with marked increases occurring from two to six years of age (e.g., Carlson et al., 2005) and continued growth at a moderate rate throughout childhood (Lengua, 2006; Lensing & Elsner, 2018; Poon, 2018). A critical milestone involves a shift away from reliance on the alerting attention network, which is primarily externally driven (e.g., responding to salient visual and auditory cues, like a sudden loud noise; Posner et al., 2012; Rothbart et al., 2003), to a more flexible executive-attention network, including the anterior cingulate cortex (ACC), basal ganglia, and areas of the PFC under dopamine modulation, with which attention becomes more internally driven and goal-directed. This shift in the dominance of attention systems is accompanied by physical maturation of brain structures, network connectivity changes, and a shift in predominant neurotransmitters involved, supporting advanced self-regulation (Rothbart et al., 2003). The executive network provides the foundation for control of working memory, monitoring conflict and conflict resolution, response to error, and selecting preferred responses between alternative options (e.g., Posner et al., 2012; Rothbart et al., 2003).

Studies link effortful control with brain activation in several domains. In a meta-analysis, EEG alpha power, a measure of engagement in self-regulatory processes, was related to executive functions in infants and young children (Hofstee et al., 2022). Parent-reported effortful control in four- to five-year-old children was related to better performance on a cognitive flexibility task and less activation of the dorsolateral PFC (Quiñones-Camacho et al., 2019). In children aged six and older, as well as in young adults, N2 and P3 event-related potential (ERP) components reflect activity in the ACC and PFC and represent executive attention and inhibitory control. Recognition of conflict or the inhibition of a prepotent response is reflected in N2 (Buss et al., 2011; Zordan et al., 2008), and P3 is related to attentional monitoring and evaluation of stimuli (e.g., Rueda et al., 2004). In middle childhood, the development of effortful control is linked with the maturation of resting state networks, in particular the default-mode (DMN) and task-positive networks (TPN). The DMN has been proposed to play a critical role in preplanned behaviors, executive behavior, and reward processing, and the TPN is important for behavioral control. Development of these systems appears to be a prerequisite for the development of attentional and behavioral control (Knyazev et al., 2017).

The implications of activity in these neural systems for children's social, emotional, and behavioral adjustment might be accounted for by the interplay between executive and emotion processes. Both hyper- and hypo-arousal of reactivity systems are associated with lower attentional and affective control (Wass, 2021). Greater relative right-frontal cortical activity is associated with withdrawal motivation and negative affect, but it is also associated with greater regulatory control (Gable et al., 2018), and greater relative right activation may be associated with effortful control of emotions rather than negative affectivity itself (Lacey et al., 2020). Neural activity related to greater executive control is expected to underlie regulation of emotional reactions, particularly negative emotions, by facilitating attentional shifting away from threatening stimuli, inhibitory control of cognitive biases, and minimizing prepotent or impulsive cognitive and behavioral responses, particularly in response to stressful experiences and contexts.

2.3.6 HPA Axis

Activity of the stress-sensitive HPA system has been linked with temperament, with the primary focus on modulating the effects of exposure to stress (e.g., Gunnar et al., 2003). Activation of the HPA axis results in the release of cortisol, and minimally invasive procedures allow for its measurement, making cortisol the most frequently studied component of the psychobiology of stress responsiveness. The HPA axis displays a diurnal rhythm with the highest levels of cortisol typically occurring in the morning and decreasing across the day, with the lowest levels near bedtime (Kirschbaum et al., 1990). Laboratory-induced stressors have been used widely to examine HPA reactivity through measuring cortisol prior to and again following an experimental manipulation in research with infants, children, and adults. Research has also leveraged changes in the diurnal cortisol rhythm in response to stressors encountered in everyday life to understand HPA functioning and the role of temperament in stress responses – for example, at the beginning of the school day (Turner-Cobb et al., 2008).

In preschool-age children, higher surgency and lower effortful control were associated with elevated cortisol, with aggressive behaviors and peer rejection mediating this association (Gunnar et al., 2003). Specifically, more surgent children with lower effortful control tended to exhibit more aggression; this translated into peer rejection, which was in turn linked with higher cortisol levels. Low positive emotionality was also associated with higher morning cortisol for preschool-age children whose mothers reported a history of depression (Dougherty et al., 2009). Spinrad et al. (2009) measured salivary cortisol levels in preschoolers before and after a frustrating task. Engaging in the task resulted in an elevation of cortisol for a portion of the preschool sample (52 percent) and higher cortisol reactivity scores – the difference between cortisol levels at pretest and at the end of the laboratory visit (approximately forty minutes posttest). These patterns were associated with greater mother-reported effortful control.

Stressful experiences, such as child maltreatment, influence the development of stress-responsive neurobiological systems, especially if the stressful experiences occur during periods of rapid brain development (Loman & Gunnar, 2010; Shannon et al., 1998). Lower socioeconomic status (SES) is associated with both elevated and blunted diurnal cortisol patterns in children and adolescents (Dowd et al., 2009), suggesting that either form of altered HPA-axis functioning may indicate a disrupted or inflexible stress-response system (Blair et al., 2011; Bruce et al., 2009).

Importantly, consistently high levels of cortisol are thought to have detrimental effects on the functioning of the HPA system by damaging the regulatory mechanism which appears to lose the sensitivity required for effective control, no longer increasing and decreasing concentrations dependent on environmental circumstances. In fact, long-term exposure to adversity seems to result in hypocortisolism, or consistently low levels of cortisol, attributed to this HPA dysregulation (Heim et al., 2000; Koss et al., 2016). The relation of HPA reactivity or cortisol concentrations with top-down control afforded by executive functions may be bidirectional, as high cortisol concentrations appear to disrupt the development of executive control, whereas deficient executive functions have been linked with excessive HPA reactivity (Blair et al., 2011; Lengua et al., 2020; Wagner et al., 2016). This disruption of executive function development may be one important mechanism behind the contribution of environmental adversity to poor self-regulation. Parenting has been shown to mediate the impact of adversity, especially poverty-related chronic stress, on HPA-axis functioning. For example, maternal negativity accounts for the effect of cumulative family risk on lower morning cortisol levels for preschool-age children (Zalewski et al., 2012). The latter is important because evidence of the effects of modifiable mediators, such as parenting, provides an avenue for potential prevention or early intervention, wherein, for example, parents could be supported to respond to their children with warm, sensitive, and consistent parenting behaviors.

3 Temperament, Developmental Processes, and Outcomes

Temperament is consistently shown to be a robust predictor of children's developmental outcomes, including academic and social–emotional competence, peer relationships, and behavioral and physical health outcomes. Rothbart and Bates (2007) proposed several potential processes to account for these effects, and evidence supports temperament's direct, additive, indirect, reciprocal, and interactive effects. Risk and promotive factors in children's contexts shape the biological underpinnings and behavioral manifestations of temperament. In turn, temperament influences the degree to which a child is exposed to some risk and promotive factors and contributes to the likelihood of children developing problems. Temperament also moderates relational and contextual experiences, increasing or decreasing the effects of both risk and promotive experiences.

3.1 Direct Effects

Temperament characteristics, individually and in combination, have direct and additive effects on children's developmental outcomes, often over and above the contribution of other relational and contextual influences. Temperament predicts children's academic competence and performance as well as peer relationships and social competence in school settings (e.g., Sanson et al., 2011). Negative reactivity has been linked to higher levels of both internalizing and externalizing problems (Eisenberg et al., 2002; Eisenberg et al., 2009), and effortful control predicts better social competence and lower internalizing and externalizing problems in children (e.g., Eggum-Wilkens et al., 2016; Eisenberg et al., 2004; Kim-Spoon et al., 2019; Spinrad et al., 2007; Van Beveren et al., 2019). Positive affect, when examined individually, predicts positive outcomes such as social–emotional competence (Eisenberg et al., 2009), whereas low positive affect is associated with increased risk of depression, particularly in combination with high negative emotionality (Dougherty et al., 2010). By contrast, surgency increases the risk of externalizing at high levels and of internalizing at low levels (Gartstein et al., 2012). These effects sometimes manifest as a developmental cascade from one outcome to another. For example, temperament anger reactivity in early childhood predicts lower social skills at age seven, which, in turn, predicts teacher-rated academic performance and problem behaviors (Dollar et al., 2018). Additionally, temperament contributes to health-related outcomes. For example, temperament negative affect and self-regulation relate to sleep problems in infants (Morales-Munoz et al., 2020) and in adolescents (Moore et al., 2011). Also, temperament relates to children's eating behavior, parental feeding practices, and children's weight, with relevance to children's obesity (e.g., Stifter & Moding, 2019).

3.2 Indirect, Evocative, and Reciprocal Effects

Temperament has an indirect effect on developmental outcomes through evocative effects that influence how others react to and interact with the child, including reciprocal associations, which both shape and are shaped by children's relationships and experiences (Lengua & Wachs, 2012). Multiple studies provide evidence of "child effects" – namely, child temperament being related to alterations in parenting and parent–child interactions. For example, greater propensity toward smiling and laughter and increases in these expressions of joy across the first year of life predicted fewer negative parenting practices (Bridgett et al., 2013). On the other hand, greater infant negative emotionality predicted more overall maternal parenting stress, and child anger was prospectively related to hostile parenting from adoptive parents (Shewark et al., 2021). When children's higher negative emotionality and lower effortful control elicit more negative parent behaviors, these parent behaviors, in turn, can increase children's vulnerable temperament characteristics (e.g., Eisenberg et al., 1999; Klein et al., 2018; Lengua, 2006). For example, infant irritability predicted less effective stimulation and physical contact, less responsiveness, and more sooth-ing behaviors compared to mothers of nonirritable infants (van den Boom & Hoeksma, 1994), whereas greater maternal responsiveness predicted decreases in irritability (van den Boom, 1989).

There is similar evidence that temperament elicits differential responses from other adults in children's lives, such as teachers. For example, child shyness and effortful control were shown to both directly and indirectly predict teacher–child conflict and closeness, and in particular, child shyness was indirectly related to lower teacher–child closeness through less frequent child-initiated teacher–child interactions (Rudasill & Rimm-Kaufmann, 2009). Indirect effects are also reflected in children's selection of experiences and environments (e.g., Caspi & Shiner, 2008). For example, negative emotionality and low effortful control predict selection into deviant peer groups (e.g., Clark et al., 2023; Creemers et al., 2010).

The association of temperament with children's social, emotional, and behav-ioral outcomes might also be indirect through its impact on appraisal and coping responses to stress (Carson & Bittner, 1994; Lengua et al., 1999; Santiago et al., 2012; Thompson et al., 2014), which, in turn, mediate the effects of tempera-ment on adjustment (Thompson et al., 2014). Individual differences in reactivity and self-regulation contribute to the individual's initial automatic response to stress and may constrain or facilitate certain types of regulatory processes, particularly higher-order appraisal and coping characteristics such as the ability to sustain and shift attention toward or away from a stressor, baseline levels of arousal, and the ability to use strategies to deal with negative emotions (Compas et al., 2001, 2004; Evans & Kim, 2012). Indeed, temperament predicts rank-order changes in appraisal and coping, with effortful control predicting relative decreases in threat appraisal and frustration predicting relative decreases in active coping (Thompson et al., 2014).

3.3 Interaction Effects

Interactive effects involve temperament altering the magnitude or direction of effects of relational and contextual factors, such as exacerbating or mitigating the effects of parenting, family, neighborhood, or SES-related risk. For example, individual differences in sensitivity to threat, affective arousal in the face of stress, and capacity for regulating cognitive, emotional, and behavioral responses to stress can either increase or decrease the impact of other risk factors, thus contributing to the likelihood of vulnerable or resilient outcomes. A variety of patterns of temperament-by-environment interactive effects have been hypothesized and observed. Goodness-of-fit refers to the degree of match between the child's characteristics and the parent's demands, expectations, or behaviors. That is, a good match between a child's temperament and his or her environment (parenting in particular) leads to more positive adjustment, whereas a poor fit between child characteristics and the demands of their surroundings leads to problematic or maladaptive outcomes (Thomas & Chess, 1977). The differential reactivity model proposes that children with different individual characteristics vary in their reactivity to both environmental stressors and supports (Wachs, 1992). The diathesis–stress framework, articulated by Heim and Nemeroff (1999) and elsewhere, specifies that poor or adverse experiences will be most detrimental to those with certain vulnerability traits that exacerbate the negative effects of exposure to such experiences. However, the diathesis–stress model does not offer hypotheses about individual differences in response to positive or supportive experiences. Differential susceptibility (Boyce & Ellis, 2005) and vantage sensitivity models (Pluess, 2017) represent special cases of differential reactivity. In the differential susceptibility model, it is theorized that traits associated with gene variants that increase an individual's vulnerability when exposed to a low-quality environment also increase their responsiveness to the positive effects of the corresponding high-quality environment (Boyce & Ellis, 2005). The vantage sensitivity model specifies that gene variants associated with increased vulnerability to adversity also increase the likelihood that individuals will benefit from supportive environmental influences in general (Pluess, 2017).

The preponderance of studies examine how temperament contributes to children's adjustment and psychopathology by mitigating or exacerbating the effects of stress and adversity, thus contributing to children's vulnerable or resilient responses to stress (Lengua & Wachs, 2012). For example, one longitudinal study found that, for children high in negative emotionality at age 1½ years, cumulative risk had an increased negative impact on emotion dysregulation at age 3½ years, and in turn, emotion dysregulation predicted lower social competence at ages 5 and 6 years across both home and school contexts (Chang et al., 2012). A cross-sectional study by Corapci (2008) found that the adverse impact of cumulative risk on social competence in preschoolers was exacerbated by low inhibition, but children who were high in inhibition had comparable social competence under both low- and high-risk environments. Another study used both variable and person-centered analyses to examine the moderating effects of temperament on the association of cumulative risk with preschool-age children's teacher-reported adjustment problems, finding that children higher in frustration, lower in fear, and lower in delay ability were particularly vulnerable to developing adjustment problems in high-risk contexts (Moran et al., 2017). In a longitudinal study with a large Dutch population-based cohort, lower levels of surgency mitigated the positive association between early life stress and externalizing problems, whereas better attention shifting capacities, an aspect of executive functioning, weakened the association between early life stress and internalizing problems (de Maat et al., 2022). The findings across these studies are consistent with a diathesis–stress model wherein a temperament characteristic exacerbates the effects of a risk factor on children's adjustment, or protective effects, in which a temperament characteristic mitigates the effects of stress. A meta-analysis found that the most consistent support in interaction tests is for diathesis–stress and goodness-of-fit models (Slagt et al., 2016).

A notable gap in this literature is a lack of consideration of the mechanisms that account for the moderation of stress exposure, and this is an important direction for future research. For example, in one study the association between cumulative risk and parenting behaviors depended on children's level of self-regulation. Cumulative risk was associated with lower maternal-responsive parenting, controlling for children's temperament, and a regulated temperament (low frustration and high regulation) was associated with higher maternal responsiveness and lower maternal-control behaviors. Furthermore, the positive association between cumulative risk and maternal control was stronger for children who demonstrated a less regulated temperament (Popp et al., 2008).

In addition, individual differences in temperament might result in a differential impact of stress on appraisal and coping (Chang et al., 2012; Corapci, 2004; Dich et al., 2017). In one study, temperament moderated the association between cumulative risk and changes in appraisal and coping over time (Parrish et al., 2021). Children who are higher in effortful control show an increase in their level of positive appraisal, whereas children low in effortful control decrease their use of active coping, as levels of cumulative risk increase (Parrish et al., 2021). Overall, these findings highlight the importance of considering the mechanisms of temperament-by-context interactions, including the potential mediating roles of family relationships, parenting, and children's appraisal and coping, which are key influences on children's developmental outcomes.

Rothbart and Bates also identified temperament-by-temperament interactions as potential processes for understanding linkages between temperament and adjustment, and in particular self-regulation modulating reactivity (Nigg, 2006; Rothbart & Bates, 2007). Rothbart and Bates (2007) described regulatory systems as capable of moderating more reactive ones, so that for a distress-prone child, greater effortful control would enable more flexible, and presumably adaptive, emotional responses in comparison to a child high in negative reactivity and not presenting with high effortful control. Consistent with this theoretical formulation, Eisenberg et al. (2001) reported an interaction effect wherein greater effortful control buffered the effect of higher anger/frustration on maladjustment. Gartstein and colleagues (2012) similarly reported higher levels of both internalizing and externalizing behaviors in children with low effortful control and high negative emotionality, in comparison to distress-prone children with more advanced regulatory skills. Similar findings show that higher frustration reactivity is more strongly related concurrently and prospectively to early adolescent externalizing problems, but not anxiety or depression, when youth are lower in executive control (Halvorson et al., 2022). Youssef et al. (2016) found that negative emotional reactivity was associated with adolescent risk-taking (a composite that included substance use, multiple sexual partners, bike helmet and seatbelt use, etc.) at low levels of effortful control.

Temperament-by-temperament interactions have also been examined in relation to sensitivity to punishment and reward. Rhodes et al. (2013) used lab tasks to assess sensitivity to punishment and reward (negative and positive emotional reactivity) and inhibitory control. Results suggested that low reward sensitivity was prospectively associated with adolescent depression symptoms at high levels of inhibitory control. In contrast, high reward sensitivity was prospectively associated with high levels of externalizing problems at low levels of inhibitory control. In a cross-sectional study, Sportel et al. (2011) found that high levels of sensitivity to punishment were associated with internalizing symptoms, and this relationship was strongest at low levels of attentional control. Kim-Spoon et al. (2016) found that sensitivity to reward was associated with adolescent substance use, but only at low levels of inhibitory control assessed via a composite of behavioral task and imaging data. As in Colder et al. (2013), sensitivity to punishment was unrelated to substance use. Overall, these studies support the idea that reactivity and regulation operate together in the form of moderation to predict internalizing and externalizing problems and substance use.

The relevant relationships, experiences, and contexts that interact and transact with temperament may vary at different developmental stages, as do the processes by which temperament contributes to children's developmental outcomes. The remaining sections discuss key relationships, experiences, contexts, and processes that, together with temperament, shape children's development.

4 Social, Cultural, and Contextual Influences on Temperament Development

Although we focus on the contributions of child temperament to their developmental outcomes, it is critical to consider the broader contexts in which children and families are situated. Contextual factors often have stable or persistent effects on parents, caregivers, family relationships, neighborhood, and school experiences. In addition, culture, social expectations, and contextual stressors affect an individual's reactivity and regulation. These contextual influences must be accounted for to gain a better understanding of temperament's contribution to developmental outcomes and to avoid overestimating the effects of child temperament. For example, in the presence of persistent or pervasive contextual influences that potentially contribute to higher levels of negative emotionality or lower effortful control, the context may function as a third variable or confounding factor that accounts for a substantial portion of the association between temperament and developmental outcomes. Furthermore, the adaptive functions of a temperament trait depend on the cultural norms, values, and attitudes toward that trait in the specific cultural context. For example, the relation between shyness and social competence was found to vary between North American and Chinese cultures, between rural and urban Chinese children, and between cohorts of urban Chinese children in different phases of social change (Yiu et al., 2020).

4.1 Culture, Immigration Status, and Acculturation

Culture plays a role in variations in the development and manifestation of temperament characteristics. This transmission of culture is thought to occur via the developmental niche, a child's proximal environment including settings and experiences (Harkness & Super, 1994; Super & Harkness, 1986). Culture shapes physical and social settings, child-rearing practices and socialization goals, and parental "ethnotheories," that is, values and beliefs about socialization practices that will facilitate the goals of child development. Furthermore, the contextual-developmental perspective asserts that cultural differences in values and expectations around emotionality, self-regulation, and social interactions can shape attitudes toward children's temperament and result in differential reinforcement or approval of desired characteristics and rejection of less-desired characteristics, which in turn shapes temperament development and expression and its functional significance (Chen, 2018). Culture-level values such as collectivism and individualism have also been linked with temperament development (Putnam & Gartstein, 2017). Individualism depicts a cultural emphasis on self-interest and preservation, with relatively loose social networks, whereas collectivism refers to an emphasis on group success and strong social connectedness (Hofstede et al., 2010).

These perspectives are revealed in cultural variation in characteristics such as shyness and self-regulation. For example, independence and initiative are viewed as valuable goals of socialization in Western, individualistic societies, but are less desirable in Eastern societies that may be more collectivistic. Thus, higher levels of shyness and fearfulness are associated with positive parental and family responses in China, South Korea, and Thailand, compared with families in Canada, the United States, and Australia (e.g., Chen et al., 1998; Kim et al., 2008; Rubin et al., 2006). Similarly, self-regulation is emphasized in collectivistic cultures, as they are more likely to encourage engagement in behaviors that benefit the common good. Therefore, parents in China have stronger expectations for self-control in their children than their counterparts in North America (Chen et al., 2003). Consistent with these expectations, differences in some characteristics have been identified, although reporter biases might play a role in identified differences (Bornstein & Cote, 2009). Higher levels of self or effortful control have been found among children from East Asian societies compared to Western cultures (e.g., Chen et al., 1998; Krassner et al., 2017). And higher levels of fearfulness and self-control have been found among children from Latin American cultures, which tend to value collectivism, compared to the United States, although this relation varied by Latin American region (Gudiño & Lau, 2010; Polo & Lopez, 2009). One study utilized data from 83,847 parent reports of temperament surgency, negative affectivity, and regulatory capacity in infants, toddlers, and children from 341 samples gathered in 59 countries (Putnam et al., 2024). Negative affectivity was higher in southern Asia and South America, where countries share a more collectivistic orientation, compared to Northern and Western Europe, countries in which children who demonstrated higher surgency were more likely to be characterized by a short-term orientation, emphasizing satisfaction of immediate desires (Hofstede et al., 2010).

Cultural influences can be observed in research with children and families who immigrate to the United States. The population of children in immigrant families (i.e., children with at least one foreign-born parent) is growing rapidly around the world. In the United States, one in every four children aged 0–18 years grows up in immigrant families (Urban Institute, 2019). Yet, there are vast differences among immigrant families in terms of their reasons for migration, length, timing, path, and experiences of migration/immigration, their premigration and postmigration socioeconomic and sociocultural characteristics, as well as the attitudes, policies, and resources of immigrants' receiving countries, societies, and communities (Bornstein, 2017). According to the integrated risk and resilience model (Suárez-Orozco et al., 2018), the adaptation of immigrant-origin children is influenced by the complex interplay and interactions among individual factors (including child temperament), microsystems (e.g., family, school, neighborhood), political and societal contexts of reception, and children's developmental stage and its associated tasks.

A developmental process salient for immigrant-origin children is acculturative stress due to immigration experience and adapting to the host/dominant culture (Romero & Piña-Watson, 2017). For example, research conducted with US immigrants has highlighted multiple sources of acculturative stress, including intergroup discrimination, language stress and language brokering, intragroup marginalization, and family cultural conflict. Acculturative stress is a salient risk factor for mental health problems in children of immigrant families (Romero & Piña-Watson, 2017). By contrast, the process of immigration and cultural adaptation is often associated with unique developmental experiences such as bilingualism, biculturalism, and multiculturalism, which can be promotive or protective factors for children of immigrant families (Suárez-Orozco et al., 2016), and temperament might confer added protection or risk in relation to the process of cultural adaptation.

Research on children of immigrant families has investigated how processes of cultural orientation or acculturation might shape the development of temperament or personality (Bornstein, 2017). Cultural orientations reflect the processes by which individuals are influenced and actively engaged in the traditions, norms, values, and practices of a culture of destination (Tsai & Chentsova-Dutton, 2002). Consistent with the hypothesis that a culturally favored temperament trait would be more encouraged in immigrant families which are highly engaged in the specific cultures (e.g., effortful control is highly valued in collective cultures such as Mexican and Chinese cultures), researchers found that in Mexican-American youth, Mexican cultural values were positively associated with their effortful control in middle childhood (Atherton et al., 2019). Moreover, parents' Asian orientation was found to be positively associated with Asian-American children's regulated shyness (reflecting higher effortful control) but not temperamental shyness (Xu & Krieg, 2014). However, other researchers have failed to find direct associations between cultural orientation(s) and effortful control (Gys et al., 2024). In addition, Gys et al. (2024) found that children in immigrant families with greater parent–child gaps in Chinese orientation scored lower on parent-rated self-regulation. This finding suggests the need to consider cultural orientation in immigrant families as multigenerational and multidimensional processes and demonstrates differential associations between cultural factors and temperament traits assessed with different methods or in different contexts (Bornstein, 2017).

Research has also addressed how cultural orientation, acculturative stress, or other immigration-related processes shape the adaptive functions of temperament. Mixed evidence has been found. For example, Mexican cultural values did not moderate prospective relations between effortful control and school behavioral problems in a longitudinal study of Mexican-origin youth in the

United States (Atherton et al., 2019). Neither parents' nor children's US American and Chinese cultural orientations moderated prospective relations of self-regulation to behavioral maladjustment in a longitudinal study of Chinese-American children in early elementary school (Gys et al., 2024). However, mothers' cultural orientations moderated the relation between temperament profiles in infancy and behavioral and physiological regulation in toddlerhood in a sample of low-income, predominantly first-generation Mexican-American families (Lin et al., 2021). Specifically, a negative reactive, low-regulated temperament profile only conferred later risks for dysregulation among infants whose mothers displayed very low levels of a US American orientation (i.e., for behavioral dysregulation) or very high levels of Mexican orientation (i.e., for RSA).

4.2 Economic Hardship and Contextual Risk

Living in a context characterized by low income or poverty can take a toll on family and caregiving relationships and, in turn, on children's social, emotional, and behavioral adjustment. Some of this impact appears to be mediated by adversity on children's emotional reactivity and regulation. Approximately 14 to 18 percent of children in the United States live in poverty; however, the rates are as high as double that for Black or African American, Indigenous, Latin American, and other children of color (Kids Count Data Center, 2022). Low income is associated with the increased likelihood of a number of risk factors, including negative life events, residential instability, food insecurity, and neighborhood problems. According to the family stress model (Conger et al., 1994), these factors, in turn, can adversely impact children's family contexts, increasing the likelihood of family conflict, disorganization, and parental mental health problems. Furthermore, these risk factors often co-occur and have cumulative effects on children's adjustment (Ackerman et al., 2004; Evans, 2003; Linver et al., 2002; Mistry et al., 2002). In addition, low income and its associated risk factors can tax parental capacities for self-regulation and be related to less effective parenting, which also mediates the effects of income on children's developmental outcomes (Conger et al., 2002; McLoyd, 1990).

In particular, low income and its associated adversity shape the underlying neurobiology and behavioral expression of children's temperament. In a sample of mothers living in a low-income context, prenatal stressful life events predicted higher RSA reactivity and weaker recovery when infants were six months of age, whereas mothers' perceptions of stress predicted their reports of lower self-regulation (Bush et al., 2017). Similarly, prenatal experience of economic insecurity predicts infant RSA baseline at 2–4 months of age (Thompson et al., n.d.), and prenatal cumulative risk is related to higher infant HPA-axis reactivity (Thompson et al., 2024). The impact of income and adversity on children's temperament persists into early and middle childhood with evidence that family income or SES and its related adversity (e.g., Gouge et al., 2020; Lengua, 2006; Lengua et al., 2015; McCormick et al., 2014), as well as neighborhood SES (McCormick et al., 2014), predict higher reactivity and lower effortful control. Income, economic insecurity, and cumulative risk also relate to ERPs reflecting executive control (e.g., Kishiyama et al., 2009; Ruberry et al., 2017; Stevens et al., 2009) and dysregulation of the HPA axis in early and middle childhood (Thompson et al., 2018; Zalewski et al., 2016). Some of these effects may be accounted for by the associations of low income with experiences of neighborhood risk (e.g., high crime rates, limited recreational opportunities), family contexts and relationships, parenting, disrupted sleep, higher body mass index (BMI), and other health indicators.

4.3 Parental Mental Health

Parental mental health problems represent a context that can affect parenting, parent–child relationships, and other family relationships, as well as potentially shaping temperament. Most research examining the association of parental mental health and child outcomes has focused on maternal mental health, and both maternal depression and anxiety are associated with social, emotional, and behavioral problems in children (e.g., Barker et al., 2011; Behrendt et al., 2020; Goodman et al., 2011). One mechanism of these effects might be through effects on temperament. For example, a meta-analysis revealed that both maternal and paternal depression and anxiety are associated with greater infant negative affectivity (Spry et al., 2020), and other research indicates that they are associated with lower effortful control and positive affect, and higher surgency (e.g., Behrendt et al., 2020; Thompson et al., 2021), including in adolescence (Abitante et al., 2022). In addition, parenting and family context moderate associations of maternal depression and anxiety with temperament. For example, in a sample of infants, maternal depression predicted increases in infant temperament difficulty at low, but not at high, levels of positive family functioning (e.g., Parade et al., 2018). As noted, parental depression is more likely when families experience economic hardship and contextual risk, highlighting a central tenet of the bioecological systems model that complex, bidirectional, and interacting relations exist among children's broader social and family contexts, relationships, and temperament, and may differ at different developmental periods.

4.4 Prenatal Environment

The effects of contextual risk on children's development begin in the prenatal period. The prenatal environment shapes temperament development through epigenetic mechanisms, with pathways that involve maternal physiology and offspring brain development (Gartstein & Skinner, 2018). Stress and maternal distress experienced in gestation alter offsprings' organs, tissues, and systems, resulting in lifelong observable changes to physiology, cognition, and behavior (e.g., Van den Bergh et al., 2020) and are associated with greater infant negative emotionality and lower effortful control (e.g., Davis et al., 2007; Nolvi et al., 2016). Exposure to alcohol (e.g., Alvik et al., 2011; Haley et al., 2006; Schoeps et al., 2018), cigarettes (e.g., Froggatt et al., 2020), toxins such as lead, dichlorodiphenyltrichloroethane (DDT), polychlorinated biphenyls (PCBs), and bisphenol A (BPA) (e.g., Antonelli et al., 2016), and nutritional deficits (e.g., de Rooij et al., 2011), particularly iron deficiency (e.g., Hernández-Martíenz et al., 2011; Wachs et al., 2008), have also been shown to relate to more difficult temperament and greater negative reactivity. However, because prenatal effects on children's development often co-occur with postnatal risk factors such as maternal mental health, substance use, or economic hardship, it is important to account for persistent and pervasive contextual risk factors when investigating the potentially unique influences of the prenatal environment (e.g., Thompson et al., 2024).

5 Developmental Periods, Contexts, and Outcomes

Temperament represents core motivational and emotional reactivity and regulation systems, which are present from birth, and thus plays a role in altering relationships and experiences from birth. Infants and toddler temperament is influenced by experiences of caregiving, family relationships, and contexts, while simultaneously evoking variations in those experiences. In this period, caregiving experiences serve to regulate early childhood emotional reactivity, shaping later emerging self-regulation capacities. In the preschool and early school years, the child's environments and relationships widen to include relationships with extended family, caregivers and teachers outside the family, as well as early peer interactions. During this time, there is a marked increase in self-regulation capacities, largely driven by the development of the prefrontal cortex underlying executive function abilities. With these increased capacities for focused attention, inhibitory control, flexibility, and delay of gratification, children are introduced to more structured and formal educational contexts during middle childhood. These contexts also expand the importance and impact of social relationships with teachers, coaches, and peers, while parent and family relationships and parenting continue to have pronounced effects on children's developmental outcomes. The balance of influence from parents and families to peers, school, and community settings begins to shift in preadolescence and into adolescence, with the child's experiences increasingly involving peer, school, extracurricular, and neighborhood contexts. Through these evolving relationships and experiences outside of the home, temperament is shaped while simultaneously altering the nature and influence of those experiences on children's social, emotional, and behavioral adjustment, as well as the development of personality.

5.1 Infancy and Early Childhood

5.1.1 Fear Reactivity and Emerging Effortful Control

Many important developmental milestones are achieved in the first two years of life. With regard to aspects of temperament reactivity and regulation, fear development at the end of the first year and the emergence of attention-based regulation in the second year are likely two of the most critical. Both developmental processes are context dependent, with family and parenting factors playing a role in shaping their unfolding.

There are normative increases in fear in infancy, particularly during the latter half of the first year of life, as inhibition of approach toward novel or intense stimuli emerges (Carranza et al., 2000; Rothbart, 1986, 1988). Growth modeling studies indicate nonlinear increases in fearfulness across infancy (Braungart-Rieker et al., 2010; Gartstein et al., 2018). These intensive longitudinal evaluations of behavioral fear provide evidence of a rapid increase between eight and ten months of age, which is consistent with earlier studies (Rothbart, 1988). Individual variation in growth in fear related to temperament differences have implications for later outcomes. For example, steeper increases in fearfulness are associated with greater toddler anxiety (Gartstein et al., 2010). In addition, inhibited temperament in the second year of life predicts increased social anxiety in adolescence (Schwartz et al., 1999), and "high reactive" infants demonstrated a greater functional magnetic resonance imaging (fMRI) signal response in the amygdala to a presentation of novel faces (associated with anxiety) two decades later (Schwartz et al., 2003).

The regulatory domain of temperament is typically conceptualized as effortful control (Bridgett et al., 2015; Gartstein et al., 2016). Origins of effortful control coincide with maturation of the frontal lobes and advances in executive functions. According to Rothbart (2011), effortful control is based on the development of the executive-attention system and provides children with self-regulation and flexibility to approach objects or situations that elicit fear, or to avoid others that appear rewarding, as needed. Characteristics reflective of effortful control (e.g., flexible, voluntary control of attention, inhibitory control) are associated with development of the executive-attention system (Spinrad et al., 2007). Whereas the orienting attention network dominant during early infancy is modulated by the cholinergic system, the executive-attention network begins to exert its influence at the end of the first year of life and is primarily moderated by dopaminergic input from the ventral tegmental area (Posner et al., 2012). A number of conceptual distinctions have been made in regard to emotion regulation, and effortful control is understood to broadly support such efforts, be they focused on modulating emotion itself or on its outward expression starting at the end of the first year of life (Eisenberg et al., 2004; Rothbart, 2011).

Earlier regulatory capacity dependent on orienting attention sets the stage for development of effortful control (Gartstein et al., 2013; Putnam et al., 2008). Specifically, infants who persist in attending to stimuli, as well as soothe more easily in response to parental efforts, enjoy physical contact with caregivers and more low-intensity activities or stimuli, and show more advanced flexible and voluntarily controlled attentional skills associated with executive functions. Approach and avoidance tendencies have also been implicated in the development of effortful control and the establishment of closely linked executive functions. According to Kochanska and Knaak (2003), fearfulness may facilitate the development of effortful control. However, a negative relation between executive functions and shyness has been demonstrated (Blankson et al., 2011), suggesting a complex pattern of effects mixed in direction, with positive and negative associations between fear/shyness and executive functions contributing to effortful control. Approach-related findings also lack consistency, insofar as infant surgency is linked with higher effortful control; however, surgency at eighteen months predicts later effortful control in the negative direction (Gartstein et al., 2009; Putnam et al., 2008). This pattern of results could be a function of not adequately capturing dynamic developmental processes or the components of surgency operating differently. The variability may also be a function of moderation effects conferred by parenting, which alter the nature of approach and avoidance links with effortful control.

5.1.2 Parent–Infant Interactions and Relationship

Parent–infant interactions represent a critical aspect of the infant's social milieu that contributes to the development of effortful control and self-regulation. The brain undergoes dramatic changes during the first years of life, including an overproduction of synapses followed by pruning. The synapses that remain are thought to be experience-dependent (Kolb, 2018), and parents play a central role in structuring infants' experiences, including social interactions. Bernier et al. (2016) found that maternal positive affect was associated with EEG markers relevant to cognitive and emotional functioning, namely, higher baseline frontal theta (4–6 Hz) and alpha (6–9 Hz) at ten and twenty-four months of age. Importantly, maternal positive affect was observed at five months of age, at which time links between brain development and maternal behavior had not emerged. This "sleeper" effect likely reflects the accumulation of parent–infant interaction influences on the child's brain over time and underscores the need to investigate relations between parent–infant exchanges and children's brain development longitudinally. As noted, parent–child interactional factors, critical because of their ubiquitous nature, can be expected to moderate links between approach/avoidance and emerging regulation in infancy and across early childhood, modulating their contributions to the development of top-down control enabled by executive function. The dynamics driven by these factors are experienced on a daily basis over "multiple trials" shaping developmental changes that serve to establish self-regulation and related processes.

Parent–child interactions represent critical contributors to the development of approach and avoidance systems and their affective components (Buss & Kiel, 2013; Fox et al., 2001), with most studies examining parental sensitivity or responsiveness. For example, infants with more sensitive mothers show slower increases in fear between four and sixteen months of age (Braungart-Rieker et al., 2010). High infant reactivity to novelty predicts toddler anxiety when mothers are less sensitive at six months of age (Crockenberg & Leerkes, 2006). Maternal sensitivity also appears to serve a protective function relative to fear and right-frontal activation early in infancy (e.g., Hardin et al., 2021). Glöggler and Pauli-Pott (2008) found that children of more sensitive mothers engaged in greater active regulation in a fear-eliciting situation, which could explain this protective effect. With respect to other elements of mother–infant interactions, reciprocity has been linked with slower increases in fearfulness across the first year of life, and the tempo of interactions with lower levels of fear at four months (Gartstein et al., 2018). In examining approach systems, reciprocity and positive emotional tone of mother–infant interactions predict positive affectivity in four-month-old infants, whereas tempo of interactions is associated with steeper growth of positive affectivity across infancy (Gartstein et al., 2018).

Protective effects of sensitive, responsive parent–child interactions have been noted with respect to fear and avoidance. However, these effects do not appear to be uniform. Sensitivity to distress and nondistress both appear to be protective earlier in infancy (Leerkes et al., 2009, 2012). However, maternal sensitivity to distress tends to promote later fearful behavior, as older infants exhibiting behavioral inhibition are more likely to remain inhibited when mothers are consistently sensitive to their negative affect (Arcus, 2001; Buss & Kiel, 2013). Similarly, Park et al. (1997) reported that sensitive, nonintrusive parenting contributed to increased fearfulness for infants high in negative emotionality, and oversolicitious maternal behavior to increased inhibition for already-fearful children (Rubin et al., 2006). Highly responsive mothers, who are not intrusive or overprotective, may nonetheless inadvertently decrease opportunities for internal modulation of affect by externally regulating infant distress; this is more critical later in infancy as flexible attention-based self-regulation begins to emerge (Posner et al., 2012). The most convincing evidence that excessive sensitivity facilitates rather than dampens behavioral inhibition, increasing the risk of anxiety, comes from work with toddlers that examined maternal reactions to fear displays (Buss & Kiel, 2011; Kiel & Buss, 2012). Moderate levels of maternal sensitivity may be optimal, as both very high and low levels are likely to increase anxiety-related risk for children already demonstrating considerable fearfulness (e.g., Buss & Kiel, 2013).

Although maternal contributions to temperament development have been studied most extensively in infancy, other family members, of course, play a role as well. Fathers and extended family, as well as broader community structures including day-care facilities, provide important support for early social–emotional development. Mothers and fathers have been described as providing similar temperament ratings across the first year of life (Sechi et al., 2020), and there is also evidence that symptoms of anxiety and depression for mothers and fathers have similar associations with greater infant negative emotionality (e.g., Sechi et al., 2020). However, some mother–father differences are notable. For example, Ventura and Stevenson (1986) reported that the temperament ratings of one parent accounted for less than 50 percent of variance in the other parent's scores. In that study, mothers described their infants as more soothable and less fearful than fathers described them. Sechi et al. (2020) also identified differences in maternal and paternal ratings of infant temperament, with mothers reporting more motor activity compared to fathers at three months of age, whereas at twelve months mothers perceived their infants as higher in positive affectivity compared to fathers. Fathers may be more influenced by their child's gender than mothers when providing temperament ratings (Bayly & Gartstein, 2013; Parade & Leerkes, 2008) and may also respond differentially to child temperament attributes in terms of their parenting (Padilla & Ryan, 2019). Whereas mothers appeared less sensitive, more intrusive, and more detached with children who scored low in sociability, fathers unexpectedly engaged in more educational activities with children higher in negative emotionality.

The quality of paternal interactions with young children depends on broader paternal involvement as well as child temperament (Cerniglia et al., 2014). Specifically, a better quality of father–infant interactions was associated with greater involvement overall, but only in the context of higher child social orientation. Mehall et al. (2009) reported that marital satisfaction mediated the association between infant regulation and parental involvement, contemporaneously for mothers and longitudinally for fathers. It was noted that fathers begin to engage with their children later in infancy, and contextual factors such as marital quality become more important over time, impacting the level of their involvement.

Another important domain of the parent–child relationship has to do with the development of secure attachment – linked with more sensitive and responsive parent–child interactions (Ainsworth, 1979) and shown to predict a number of important child outcomes, such as social competence (Goldsmith & Harman, 1994). There is a modest association between negative temperament (negative emotional reactivity) and infants' attachment security with mothers, with an insecure attachment characterized by resistance being more strongly related to temperament than secure or avoidant attachment (Groh et al., 2017). No significant association was found between negative temperament and father–child attachment (Groh et al., 2017). Multiple intervention approaches for enhancing sensitivity and responsiveness in parent–child interactions are available. Some of these approaches target infants high in negative emotionality in particular, as these children have been shown to be at an increased risk of insecure attachment (Calkins & Fox, 1992). An early example of such an approach was implemented by van den Boom (1995), who delivered a brief intervention to mothers with infants high in irritability to enhance mothers' sensitivity and responsiveness to their cues. This intervention not only increased the security of attachment for participating infants, it resulted in lasting benefits, with improved child cooperation and peer interactions in later years (van den Boom, 1995). In another study, an intervention aimed at enhancing infant secure attachment had moderated effects such that the intervention had the intended effect for highly irritable infants only, indicating a particular benefit of sensitive, responsive parenting to irritable infants' attachment security (Cassidy et al., 2011).

5.1.3 Family Relationships

Infant temperament has also been examined in a broader family context, although this work has been somewhat limited to date. In one study, three-and-a-half-month-old infants' temperamental characteristics (fussiness and unadaptability) were assessed along with marital satisfaction and co-parenting behaviors

(Schoppe-Sullivan et al., 2007). Associations between infant temperament and co-parenting behaviors varied as a function of marital quality, so that for families with high marital quality more optimal co-parenting was observed in the context of a challenging temperament profile, whereas at low levels of marital quality co-parenting behavior when caring for a challenging infant was less effective.

Wong et al. (2009) examined parental beliefs about the importance of the paternal caregiving role, infant temperament, and marital quality as predictors of attachment security with both parents, after accounting for their sensitivity. For mothers, describing the paternal caregiving role as important was associated with less secure attachment, but only at high levels of infant fussiness. For fathers, the pattern of results was different: Their view of the paternal caregiving role as important was associated with a greater likelihood of having securely attached infants when levels of infant fussiness or marital quality were also rated as high. Child effects in this context are also notable; for example, mothers and fathers of infants with greater regulatory capacity express higher levels of marital satisfaction (Mehall et al., 2009). There is also evidence that fathers are more engaged in parenting when their daughters are higher in sociability (McBride & Mills, 1993) and their sons are described as "easy" in terms of their temperament (Manlove & Vernon-Feagans, 2002). A more nuanced understanding of the role of temperament in early childhood development is obtained when multiple family relationships are considered simultaneously.

5.1.4 Childcare

Temperament-related effects have also been studied in the context of early childcare experiences. Watamura et al. (2003) showed that, while children cared for in their homes typically demonstrated decreases in cortisol levels from morning to afternoon, in a day-care setting cortisol levels increased for many infants and toddlers. Importantly, those described as higher in social fear compared to less fearful children exhibited elevated afternoon cortisol and larger cortisol increases across the day in a childcare setting. Other studies have taken advantage of the childcare context to examine whether children with different temperament profiles would be differentially susceptible to the quality of caregiving effects. Pluess and Belsky (2009) reported that, compared to toddlers lower in negative emotionality, toddlers higher in negative emotionality exhibit more behavior problems and less social competence in low-quality childcare but fewer behavior problems and greater social competence in high-quality childcare settings. This pattern of results is consistent with the "for better and for worse" differential susceptibility hypothesis, wherein children with more challenging profiles perform poorly under conditions of adversity, yet demonstrate superior outcomes when exposed to enriched environments. However, such support has not been uniformly found across relevant studies. For example, contrary to expectations, children low in self-regulation (i.e., demonstrating dysregulated behavior) were no more vulnerable to relatively low-quality day care or more susceptible to day-care effects more generally, compared to their better-regulated counterparts (Broekhuizen et al., 2015). Higher levels of shyness, frustration, and soothability predict greater social competence and better social–emotional adjustment for infants and toddlers attending Dutch day care. Although supportive interactions between caregivers and children predicted child well-being and competence, no interaction effects indicative of differential susceptibility to day-care quality were observed (Fukkink, 2022).

5.1.5 Physical Health

Temperament also contributes to important aspects of physical health, among them sleeping, feeding/eating, and risk of childhood obesity. Prior studies linking temperament to sleeping and eating/feeding in childhood have unearthed associations between temperament-related challenges and eating and sleeping problems. For example, fussy–difficult temperament is associated with sleeping problems (more frequent night wakings and difficulties settling down to sleep) at one year of age and persistent sleeping problems at two years of age (Morrell & Steele, 2003). Kelmanson (2004) reported that more distress-prone infants were more likely to have problems sleeping throughout the night and needed parental interaction more frequently before falling back asleep.

Infants described as more challenging in terms of their temperament are also more likely to have difficulties with feeding. For infants in Barbados, difficult temperament was associated with feeding difficulties and greater parental involvement during feeding (Galler et al., 2004). Infants with feeding disorders were more frequently rated as having a difficult temperament, with their caregivers describing these infants as fussy and difficult to soothe (Feldman et al., 2004). More difficult temperament and higher levels of negative emotionality (frustration in particular) are associated with higher weight in cross-sectional studies and more significant weight gain in longitudinal investigations (Carey, 1985; Darlington & Wright, 2006; Hittner et al., 2016; Niegel et al., 2007). Surgency is also related to greater weight gain and higher BMI (Burton et al., 2011).

These findings have been interpreted to mean that infants and toddlers who present caregivers with temperament challenges may be at risk of sleeping and eating problems, as well as childhood obesity. With respect to sleep, these children may be particularly resistant to bedtime routines, struggling with returning to sleep when awakened at night. For feeding, displays of distress at mealtimes may lead to less effective parental efforts, or may involve more frequent feeding and reliance on calorically dense foods in order to soothe/ lower the level of arousal, which can translate into risk of obesity. However, this literature is not entirely consistent; for example, Worobey and colleagues (2014) demonstrated that feeding frequency in infancy is not a function of difficult temperament displays.

Temperament and infant physical health may have reciprocal effects, as evidence suggests that health indicators have implications for temperament development. For example, one study showed that better sleeping behaviors in a sample of primarily Black and White infants and toddlers living in low-income homes were related to better effortful control (Bates et al., 2021). Another study showed that higher BMI was prospectively associated with lower effortful control in early childhood, mediating the effects of low income on effortful control (Tandon et al., 2015).

Taken together, the evidence consistently points to the parent–child relationship, parenting, and caregiving settings as both shaping and being shaped by infant temperament. These early relationships lay the foundation for emotional reactivity and self-regulation, as well as for social, emotional, and behavioral adjustment and physical health as children transition into middle childhood.

5.2 Middle Childhood and Preadolescence

Middle childhood and preadolescence are generally defined as between the ages of six and twelve years. They represent a key period in the development of cognitive, social, emotional, and behavioral capacities that establish the foundations of mental and physical health and academic accomplishments into adolescence and adulthood (e.g., Landry & Smith, 2010; Marceau et al., 2019). Demands and expectations on children increase during this time, coinciding with their growing capacities for self-regulation, coping, problem-solving, social responsibility, and academic competencies that, in turn, contribute to their social, emotional, and behavioral adjustment. Temperament contributes to these developmental outcomes directly and in interaction and transaction with the child's family and social and environmental contexts.

During this time, children increasingly interact with individuals and systems outside the family (i.e., school, peers, media), and parents are faced with the complex task of providing adequate guidance and support while also facilitating increased individuation. As children enter grade school, they are expected to regulate their behaviors and emotions in the classroom and work independently on their school work. Children are also navigating peer relationships both inside and outside of school, in person and on social media. These relationships become more complicated as children's opportunities to connect grow increasingly independent (e.g., Gifford-Smith & Brownell, 2003). Furthermore, relationships and interactions occur in the context of neighborhood communities and broader economic, sociopolitical, and cultural contexts that can have profound effects on the risk and protective factors in children's development.

In this developmental period, transactional and interactional processes between children's temperament and parenting, and their associated emotion regulation or behavior problems, are often carried forward from infancy and early childhood into middle childhood and preadolescence (e.g., Kim & Kochanska, 2020; Leve et al., 2019), increasing the likelihood of internalizing and externalizing problems in middle childhood. In addition, children's interactions with parents, families, teachers, and peers impact and are impacted by temperament, also contributing to internalizing, externalizing, social–emotional, and academic competence.

5.2.1 Parenting

Parenting and the parent–child relationship are key influences on children's development in middle childhood and preadolescence. There is consistent evidence of reciprocal relations between parenting and children's temperament, with temperament both shaping and being shaped by parent behaviors, supporting a transactional process (Kiff et al., 2011). With regard to children's negative emotionality, harsh, unsupportive parenting predicts higher negative emotionality (e.g., Scaramella et al., 2008), whereas warm and sensitive parenting is associated with decreases in negative emotionality (e.g., Bates & Pettit, 2007; Bates et al., 2014). At the same time, negative emotionality affects parenting. High reactivity in preschool children predicts more coercive parenting (Gölcük & Berument, 2021), and preschool "hard to manage" temperament predicts more power-assertive parenting in middle childhood, particularly when families are low in resources (parents who are younger, lower education, low income; Kim & Kochanska, 2020). In addition, inconsistent discipline is related to increases in negative emotionality in children, while child irritability predicts increases in inconsistent discipline by parents (Lengua & Kovacs, 2005). Infants classified as low reactive had mothers who were more likely to employ reasoning as a response to verbal conflict when children reached middle childhood (Hardway et al., 2013). There may be some differentiation of the relations of fear and frustration as components of negative emotionality with parenting. Fearfulness may draw for more warm and supportive parenting (Lengua, 2006), and make children easier to discipline, predicting more compliance in toddlers (Kochanska et al., 2001; van der Mark et al., 2002). In contrast, frustration appears to consistently elicit more negative parenting (Kiff et al., 2011).

Clear or consistent limit-setting (Taylor et al., 2013), scaffolding (Lengua et al., 2014), and warmth (Klein et al., 2018) support the development of effortful control. In turn, effortful control predicts parenting. Lower inhibitory control predicts increased maternal hostility (Leve et al., 2019), and higher effortful control predicts lower maternal negativity (Klein et al., 2018) and more positive parenting (Soydan & Akalin, 2022), indicating that more regulated children elicit more positive parent behaviors, leading to better developmental outcomes.

Additionally, child temperament and parenting interact to predict child outcomes, with the influence of parenting increased or decreased in magnitude, or even altered in direction, by child temperament characteristics. Child frustration tends to be related to higher levels of problem outcomes over and above parenting effects and exacerbates the effects of negative parenting, whereas effortful control generally mitigates the effects of negative parenting (e.g., Kiff et al., 2011). For example, children with low effortful control show greater externalizing symptoms in response to more punishing parenting than children with higher effortful control (Ezpeleta et al., 2019). The goodness-of-fit model provides a nuanced understanding of how temperament interacts with the environment and experiences, articulating that children benefit from environments that match their temperament (Chess & Thomas, 1991). For example, gentle discipline predicts compliance and internalization of rules for fearful but not for low-fear children (Kochanska 1995, 1997), whereas fearful temperament exacerbates the negative effects of power-assertive or harsh parenting; low-fear children, however, do not seem to be adversely affected by these parenting behaviors (e.g., Kochanska et al., 2007). Also, more inhibited children at age three who receive more structured parenting at age five show lower internalizing symptoms (Liu et al., 2019), whereas more overprotective behaviors toward fearful children predict an increase in internalizing problems (Buss et al., 2021). Additionally, children who are high in surgency or impulsivity may benefit more from parental guidance in the development of effortful control, and struggle more when they are less supported or receive less structure (Shimomaeda et al., 2023; Suor et al., 2019). Temperament alters children's responses to parent behaviors, with effective parenting varying based on child temperament.

5.2.2 Family Relationships

Family relationships, including family conflict and cohesion, as well as sibling relationships, represent key socialization experiences in middle childhood and preadolescence. Low family cohesion, that is a family's emotional bonds and sense of closeness (Goodrum et al., 2020; Haddad et al., 1991), and high family conflict disrupt family stability, straining the parent–child relationships as well as sibling–sibling relationships. Child temperament influences how a child contributes and responds to the family environment. Children with more vulnerable or difficult temperament characteristics, such as higher negative emotionality or impulsivity, might struggle to cope effectively in a context of high conflict. Preschool children with more difficult temperaments exhibit greater internalizing and externalizing problems in high-conflict families compared to children with easy temperaments, who had fewer problems regardless of level of family conflict (Tschann et al., 1996). Similarly, interparental conflict is related to children's problem behaviors for children high in irritability, but not for those low in irritability (Hentges et al., 2015). Negative emotionality also moderates the relation between family cohesion and child well-being, with children higher in negative reactivity showing lower well-being in a context of low family cohesion than children lower in negative reactivity (Myerberg et al., 2019). Family context also shapes children's temperament. For example, lower family cohesion and greater conflict predict higher levels of child fearfulness (Lucia & Breslau, 2006). Finally, children contribute to these family dynamics. For example, higher effortful control is associated with increased positive involvement and communication between parents and children, regardless of parents' level of marital satisfaction (Ato et al., 2015).

5.2.3 Siblings

Sibling relationships, which are affected by family cohesion and conflict (Brody et al., 1994; Zemp et al., 2021) and by marital hostility (Dunn et al., 1999), also relate to children's temperament (Brody et al., 1994; Stocker et al., 1989), which in turn interacts with birth order and differential parental treatment (e.g., Qian et al., 2022; Stocker et al., 1989). In older siblings, shyness is associated with more positive sibling relationships (i.e., less control and competitiveness), whereas degree of emotional upset is associated with more negative relationships (Stocker et al., 1989). In younger siblings, the degree of emotional upset is associated with a negative sibling relationship, whereas sociability is associated with less cooperation but a more positive relationship overall (Stocker et al., 1989). For both older and younger siblings, differential parental treatment directed at one sibling is related to poorer sibling relationships (e.g., Stocker et al., 1989). Furthermore, child gender may moderate associations between temperament and sibling relationships. In a sample of same-sex siblings, emotional intensity and low persistence were both associated with increased agonistic behavior between sisters, and each sibling's temperament contributed equally to this dynamic. For brothers, only the younger brother's high activity and low persistence predicted more agonistic behavior (Brody et al., 1994).

5.2.4 Neighborhood

There has been relatively little research on how neighborhood context shapes temperament in middle childhood or preadolescence. One exception is Hart et al. (2008), who used two waves of data from the child sample of the National Longitudinal Survey of Youth (National Longitudinal Surveys, n.d.), the first when children were three to four years of age, and again two years later. Neighborhood economic disadvantage was associated with children's undesirable personality/temperament change (decreases in resiliency and overcontrol and increases in undercontrol) after controlling for family-level characteristics. These investigators further tested whether maternal depression, Head Start participation, cognitive and emotional support in the home, or maternal trust in the neighborhood mediated the relation between neighborhood economic deprivation and temperament change, but no evidence of mediation was found (Hart et al., 2008). Using data from the Longitudinal Study of Australian Children (Australian Institute of Family Studies, 2015) that followed children from four to fifteen years of age, Stickhouser and Sutin (2020) examined the joint associations of family and neighborhood socioeconomic disadvantage with three temperament traits (sociability, reactivity, and persistence). After controlling for family SES, greater neighborhood disadvantage at baseline was associated with children's lower sociability and higher reactivity, and these relations were stable over time.

Temperament can moderate the impact of neighborhood context on other domains of child development. For example, using an urban community sample of eight-to-twelve-year-old children, Bush and colleagues (2010) found that neighborhood problems (measured by parent and observer ratings) were more strongly related to lower social competence for more fearful than for less fearful children and for less irritable than for more irritable children. Moreover, neighborhood social organization was more strongly associated with higher social competence for low-fear children than higher-fear children. In a sample of youth aged ten to twelve years, selected on the basis of the presence or absence of a paternal history of substance use disorder or other psychiatric disorders, Rabinowitz et al. (2016) found that youth temperamental withdrawal interacted with neighborhood processes in predicting their risks for internalizing symptoms. Specifically, youth with high withdrawal manifested higher anxiety/depressive symptoms than youth with low withdrawal in the context of low neighborhood crime but not in the context of high neighborhood crime. Youth with high withdrawal also manifested greater internalizing symptoms in the context of low neighborhood social cohesion but not in the context of high neighborhood social cohesion.

Although the patterns of temperament-by-neighborhood interactions reported in the literature have been mixed, these findings have provided evidence that temperament plays a significant role in shaping children's socialization experience in neighborhood and community contexts. Further supporting this perspective, Zhao et al. (2022) identified two longitudinal trajectories of child exposure to community violence (CECV) reflecting high exposure and low exposure to CECV, using an at-risk sample of primarily low-income families with high rates of prenatal substance exposure. Child temperament and maternal harshness interacted in predicting children's CECV trajectories: Children with high activity levels and experiencing high maternal harshness in early childhood had the highest likelihood of being in the high exposure-increasing trajectory (Zhao et al., 2022). This study illustrates the value of examining multiple system levels simultaneously, demonstrating the relevance of interactions and transactions across temperament, parenting, or family system variables, and broader contexts.

5.2.5 Peers

Because temperament emotional reactivity and regulation play central roles in the quality of children's relationships in general, it is not surprising that they impact children's peer relationships both directly, as children engage with peers differently and evoke different responses from them, and indirectly through children's social skills (Sanson et al., 2011). Social or peer competence is the ability to initiate and maintain effective interactions and relationships with peers, which promotes a sense of belonging (e.g., Rubin et al., 2009) and has implications for children's social, emotional, behavioral, and academic adjustment over time, including predicting peer problems, personality, and psychopathology into adolescence (e.g., Baardstu et al., 2020; Rapee, 2014).

Children's higher effortful control predicts better social competence (Lengua et al., 2014; Zhou et al., 2010) and lower externalizing and aggression (Zhou et al., 2010). In particular, inhibitory control and attention focusing are related to lower peer conflict, and attention focusing is related to higher sociability, better communication and assertiveness in peer interactions (Acar et al., 2015), and higher social confidence (Beceren & Özdemir, 2019) in preschool-age children. Children higher in effortful control are more likely to modulate an emotional reaction, delay an impulsive response, attend to relevant cues in the situation, and, as a result, engage in more effective efforts at initiating and maintaining interactions.

Conversely, children who are higher in negative emotionality (Brumariu & Kerns, 2013), and anger or frustration in particular (Zhou et al., 2010), tend to exhibit lower social or peer competence and higher externalizing problems, which interfere with positive peer relationships. These children react more strongly and negatively during peer interactions, particularly during disagreements or conflicts, provoking negative reactions from peers and rupturing relationships. Furthermore, a bidirectional process contributes to the development of peer problems such that being higher in negative emotionality lowers peer status, which in turn increases negative emotionality (Bengtsson et al., 2022). One mechanism that accounts for this reciprocal association is an increased tendency to perceive and expect rejection from peers (Araiza et al., 2020). Children higher in negative emotionality and lower in regulation are more likely to be rejected by peers (Ato et al., 2020). In addition, children higher in anxiety–withdrawal and anger–aggression are also more likely to experience peer victimization, particularly if they are immigrants (Pistella et al., 2020). Child inhibition or fearfulness also impacts peer relationships. For example, highly inhibited or risk-averse preschool-age children aged three to five are less socially integrated and less dominant than children who are average or highly exuberant or risk seeking, but they are not more likely to be rejected by peers (Tarullo et al. 2011). In contrast, highly exuberant children are more dominant, more often exhibit anger, and have more conflictual relationships (Tarullo et al., 2011).

Surgency, which is related to exuberance, also contributes to peer relationships. Surgency combines positive affect and impulsivity with low shyness and withdrawal, all behaviors that play a role in peer interactions. Whereas low-surgent children are likely to be shy and socially withdrawn (e.g., Rubin et al., 2009), high-surgent children are likely to be socially engaged and outgoing (Rubin et al., 1995) but are also likely to develop externalizing problems (Stifter et al., 2008) and be rejected by peers (e.g., Gunnar et al., 2003). Examining children's surgency as they were entering grade school at 6–7 years of age, one study found that children high in surgency developed more negative peer-related behaviors, including initiating and maintaining negative interactions, whereas children low in surgency demonstrated more wariness with peers (Dollar & Stifter, 2012).

It appears that these associations depend on other moderating factors, such as children's self-regulation or emotion-regulation capacities as well as the presence of supportive adults. Negative emotionality and effortful control interact in predicting social competence and peer relationship quality, with effortful control modulating the effects of emotionality (Eisenberg et al., 2002). Similar patterns of association have been found in relation to aspects of social and peer competence. For example, moderate to high levels of self-regulation predict successful social functioning, particularly for children who are also high in negative emotionality (Eisenberg et al., 2002). Attention focusing moderates the association between shyness and peer communication skills such that high shyness is related to poor communication only for children low in attention focusing. Low shyness is related to high peer conflict, but again only for children low in attention focusing (Acar et al., 2015).

Children's peer relationships most often occur in school or in other social contexts, and their relationships with parents, teachers, and other adults, such as coaches, appear to moderate associations of emotionality and self-regulation with peer relationships. For example, when children high in surgency also demonstrate support-seeking during a challenging task, they were rated as lower in aggression compared to those not seeing support (Dollar & Stifter, 2012). In addition, parenting moderates the relation of fear or inhibition in early childhood to later peer withdrawal, with sensitive or less overcontrolling parenting mitigating the association (Sanson et al., 2011). Similarly, the interaction between parenting and difficult temperament predicts social competence, such that when parental emotional and autonomy support are low, children with difficult temperament are rated by teachers as having lower social competence, but not when parenting quality is high (Straight et al., 2008).

The quality of the relationship between teachers and children moderates and mediates the relations of temperament with peer interactions (Rudasill et al., 2013). One study found that children's difficult temperament was related to less close relationships and more conflict with teachers. Teacher–child closeness was positively related to children's prosocial behaviors, and teacher–child conflict was related to high levels of aggression, victimization, and fewer prosocial interactions, with teacher–child conflict mediating the association between difficult temperament and peer behaviors (Rudasill et al., 2013). Another study found that teacher sensitivity and responsiveness in first grade, with children aged 6–7, moderated the association of infant temperament with children's first-grade peer relationships. Having a sensitive teacher buffered the disruptive effects of low approach, adaptability, and high negative affect on peer interactions (Frohn et al., 2021).

5.2.6 School and Academics

Peer relationships and teacher–child relationships are key pathways through which temperament shapes children's academic achievement and school adaptation. In addition, researchers have examined children's classroom engagement, liking school, and learning-related behaviors (e.g., study skills) as mediators in relations between temperament and academic achievement. For example, using a school-based sample of 2nd to 6th graders aged 6–12 years in Spain, Sánchez-Pérrez et al. (2018) found that children with high effortful control had better study skills, which in turn were associated with higher academic achievement and positive social adaptations at school. Furthermore, Valiente et al. (2012) found that kindergartners in the United States who were high on temperamental shyness, anger, or impulsivity and low on effortful control displayed lower school liking and classroom participation, but effortful control buffered children from the deleterious effects of impulsivity and anger on school-related outcomes. In addition, researchers have found bidirectional relations between temperament and academic achievement. For example, effortful control shows bidirectional and positive relations with children's math achievement in school-aged children 5–9 years old from Chinese-American immigrant families (Mauer et al., 2021). Together, these studies highlight the complex pathways through which temperament shapes children's learning experience and adaptations in the school context.

5.3 Adolescence

Adolescence is a period of transition from childhood to adulthood that is often considered to span the ages 12–18. This period is characterized by marked changes across multiple domains, including physical, cognitive, emotional, and social development. These changes have substantial implications for the development of temperament, temperament transactions with the environment, and the influence of temperament on adjustment and psychopathology. Here, we consider the developmental context of adolescence, and summarize some of the main themes in adolescent temperament research, including the development of temperament, relationships between temperament and adjustment, and contextual factors.

Physical development during adolescence is dramatic and culminates in the attainment of sexual maturation and adult stature. These changes impact how adolescents view themselves (e.g., self-esteem, self-concept) and how they are treated and responded to by others (Graber et al., 2010). Brain maturation during this period supports cognitive development, including increased efficiency in information processing, better integration of memory and experience, and improved abstract thinking and cognitive control (Giedd, 2012, 2015; Keating, 2012). Maturation of limbic structures is believed to increase reactivity to reward and stress, and influence processing of emotional experiences and social information (Romeo, 2012). A notable feature of adolescent brain maturation is that development of neural structures that support improvements in cognitive control is protracted relative to changes in limbic structures, which occur more rapidly. This asynchrony is believed to result in positive emotional reactivity and reward motivation that exceed the capacity for effective self-regulation and cognitive control, impacting risk-taking and problem behavior (Almy et al., 2018; Luciana & Collins, 2012; Steinberg et al., 2008).

Coinciding with physical, cognitive, and emotional changes, social relationships are transformed during adolescence. Neural development in the limbic system coupled with hormonal changes during puberty (e.g., increases in oxytocin) are implicated in heightened attentiveness to social stimuli and the increased salience of peer relations (Steinberg, 2008), supporting a shift toward spending more time with peers and increased interest in romantic relationships. These changes also impact parent–child relationships. Autonomy and independence are key developmental tasks of adolescents and require parent–child relationships to reorganize and become more egalitarian (Allen & Loeb, 2015; Branjie, 2018). Although it is important for parents to provide continued warmth, support, monitoring, and discipline, there is a general trend for parental demands or control to decline during adolescence (Keijsers & Poulin, 2013).

5.3.1 Change in Temperament

Brain development that occurs during adolescence implies that both reactivity and regulatory components of temperament change during this period (Caspi et al., 2005). Facets of positive emotional reactivity increase during adolescence, with evidence of increases in behavioral approach, reward sensitivity, and high intensity pleasure (e.g., Colder et al., 2013; Pagliaccio et al., 2016; Zohar et al., 2019). Conversely, negative emotional reactivity appears to decline during adolescence, although the literature is limited. Colder et al (2013) found that sensitivity to punishment, assessed using a laboratory task, declined from early to middle adolescence. This is consistent with evidence that parent-reported fear, frustration, and shyness declined in early to middle adolescence (Laceulle et al., 2012) and that self-reported sensitivity to punishment declined during middle adolescence (Balle et al., 2022).

Effortful control is expected to improve during adolescence as neural structures supporting cognitive control mature; however, this may depend on the specific dimensions assessed and on the measurement method. Ferguson et al. (2021)

found that task-assessed planning ability, working memory, and inhibitory control improved during adolescence, but measures of cognitive flexibility did not change. Fosco et al. (2019) used a laboratory task and parent-report questionnaire to assess inhibitory control and, consistent with Fergusson et al. (2021), found that task-assessed inhibitory control improved from early to middle adolescence. However, no change was evident for parent-reported inhibitory control. Impulsivity is often construed as an aspect of effortful control. However, it is a heterogenous construct that also often includes reward reactivity and approach motivation (Dawe et al., 2004). Impulsivity seems to increase during early adolescence, with a peak around age fifteen, and then it declines (Quin & Harden, 2013; Shulman et al., 2015). These patterns might suggest that cognitive control is initially overwhelmed by rapid development in reward reactivity and approach motivation, and that with maturity of relevant neural structures adolescents are better able to modulate positive emotional reactivity.

5.3.2 Psychopathology and Substance Use

Vulnerability models suggest that temperament can increase risk for poor adjustment and psychopathology (De Bolle et al., 2012). Poor effortful control and high negative emotional reactivity are cross-sectionally and prospectively associated with adolescent internalizing symptoms (Colder & O'Connor, 2004; de la Torre-Luque et al., 2020; Hoffmann et al., 2019; Snyder et al., 2015). Lawson et al. (2022) found that high levels of effortful control decreased the probability of adolescents experiencing the onset of suicidal ideation, plans, and attempts (a cluster of symptoms associated with depression), whereas high levels of negative emotional reactivity increased the probability of experiencing the onset of these symptoms. Poor effortful control and high positive emotional reactivity are associated with externalizing symptoms, including substance use (Colder & O'Connor, 2004; Colder et al., 2013; Fosco et al., 2019; Hoffmann et al., 2019; Snyder et al., 2015).

In a seven-year longitudinal study that spanned the ages 12–19 years, Dolcini-Catania et al. (2020) tested a mediational model whereby temperament at age twelve predicted mental health symptoms in early adolescence, which in turn predicted major depressive symptoms in late adolescence. Low surgency, high negative emotional reactivity, and low effortful control predicted internalizing, which in turn predicted symptoms of major depression. There was also support for an externalizing pathway that involved low effortful control that predicted externalizing problems, which in turn predicted symptoms of major depression. This study is notable because it suggests a cascading effect of temperament that increases vulnerability for psychopathology many years later and demonstrates that temperament impacts adjustment through multiple complex pathways consistent with the idea of equifinality (multiple pathways can lead to the same outcome).

Temperament is also related to health outcomes in adolescence. For example, Nelson et al. (2018) examined the association of adolescent temperament with C-reactive protein (CRP), which is believed to index inflammation and immune system functioning. This is of interest because high levels of CRP are linked to poor physical and mental health. Findings suggested that effortful control was associated with low levels of CRP, whereas negative emotional reactivity was associated with high levels of CRP. Brody et al. (2023) similarly found that high levels of negative emotional reactivity and poor attentional control in adolescence were associated with worsening inflammation in young adulthood. These studies suggest a potential biological pathway whereby immune functioning as measured by indicators of inflammation may mediate links between temperament and mental and physical health outcomes.

An intriguing model that might account for linkages between temperament and adjustment is the scar model, initially proposed by Lewinsohn and colleagues (1981). The model posits that experiencing intense psychopathology symptoms leaves a lasting impact on temperament, which could manifest as temporary (i.e., scab effect) (Li & Zinbarg, 2007) or long-lasting (i.e., scar effect) changes in temperament. Along with the vulnerability model, this suggests potential reciprocal associations between temperament and adjustment. In one of the few tests of this idea with a longitudinal adolescent sample, Ramer et al. (2024) found that sensitivity to reward was reciprocally associated with oppositional defiant symptoms in early and middle adolescence, such that high sensitivity to reward predicted subsequent oppositional defiant symptoms (vulnerability) and high levels of oppositional defiant symptoms predicted subsequent sensitivity to reward (scar).

Temperament influences learning, including the degree to which positive and negative reinforcement and punishment shape behavior (Shiner & Caspi, 2012), and temperament differences elicit different reactions from the environment (Bates et al., 2014). Hence, linkages between temperament and adjustment likely depend on features of the environment. In their review, Rioux et al. (2016) concluded that there was consistent evidence that high levels of substance use and externalizing behaviors in adolescence were most evident when more adverse family environments were combined with an "adventuresome temperament" (a combination of activity level and reward motivation, and low levels of effortful control, negative affect, fearfulness, and shyness). Poor regulation and strong emotional reactivity seem to leave children vulnerable to the effects of adverse family environments. Using a large longitudinal sample, Kapetanovic et al. (2023) found evidence for moderated mediational pathways predicting adolescent substance use. Positive parenting and harsh discipline were associated with adolescent substance use indirectly through sensation-seeking, and these indirect effects were moderated by adolescent temperament. The authors concluded that the study provided evidence for differential susceptibility, such that a temperament characteristic could be a liability in one parenting and family context, but protective in another. For example, poor activation control was a liability for adolescents in the context of low positive parental practices, but these adolescents were more resilient to harsh discipline.

5.3.3 Peer and Romantic Relationships

As noted, peer relationships become increasingly important in adolescence, and successful adaptation in this domain has both short- and long-term implications for a variety of psychosocial outcomes. There is evidence that temperament plays an important role in social adaptation in adolescents. Adolescent effortful control is associated with social competence, and this association is partly mediated by empathy and perspective-taking (Zorza et al., 2013; Murphy et al., 1999, 2004). A small number of studies have considered the role of temperament in youth that affiliate with deviant peers who support and encourage problem behavior. Findings suggest that poor effortful control, high intensity pleasure (an aspect of positive emotional reactivity related to novelty/sensation-seeking), and negative emotional reactivity influence selection into deviant peer groups and friendships, which in turn predict engagement in substance use and antisocial behavior (e.g., Clark et al., 2023; Creemers et al., 2010). Temperament is also likely to influence selection into prosocial peer groups and friendships, but this has been less studied and remains an important direction for future research.

Temperament might also moderate the influence of peers on adjustment outcomes. For example, affiliating with peers engaging in deviant behavior is strongly associated with antisocial behavior such as delinquency and aggression, and this relationship is particularly strong for youth characterized by poor effortful control (Mrug et al., 2012). Scalco et al. (2021) found that high surgency and low effortful control in conjunction with peer alcohol use were associated with heavy drinking in middle adolescence, which in turn was associated with alcohol-use disorder symptoms in late adolescence. Scalco and Colder (2017) found that perceived peer norms about alcohol and drug use were most strongly associated with increases in cannabis use among youth who were high in surgency. One study considered internalizing symptoms and found that peer rejection was associated with increases in adolescent depression, and this association was strongest at high levels of negative emotional reactivity (Brengden et al., 2005). Overall, these studies suggest that temperament leaves some youth particularly vulnerable to negative peer contexts.

Romantic relationships represent a domain of peer relationships that first emerge in adolescence. A small number of studies have found that temperament influences the nature and quality of adolescent romantic relationships. For example, poor effortful control in early adolescence is associated with bullying perpetration, which in turn predicted having many dating partners and dating aggression in late adolescence (Farrell & Vaillencourt, 2019). Low effortful control and high negative emotional reactivity at age seventeen was associated with problematic romantic relationships in young adulthood (Semak et al., 2020). Given that early romantic relationships help set the stage for adult romantic relationships, additional studies that consider adolescent temperament would be an important direction for research, including studies that consider the potential mechanisms of these associations.

5.3.4 Neighborhood

Neighborhoods influence child adjustment, and as youth enter adolescence they may be more susceptible to neighborhood contexts, as they are likely to venture out without adult supervision. Several studies have considered temperament within the neighborhood context. A large literature suggests that neighborhood disadvantage (neighborhoods characterized by poverty, low social cohesion, and danger) is associated with adolescent externalizing behavior and internalizing behavior. Trentacosta et al. (2009) considered the moderating effect of sensation-seeking in a sample of boys and found that neighborhood danger was associated with adolescent externalizing symptoms at high levels of sensation-seeking (referred to as "daring" by the authors). Andreas and Watson (2016) similarly found that neighborhood disadvantage was associated with increased drug use for adolescents high in sensation-seeking (also see Neumann et al., 2010). In one of the few studies of neighborhood to consider temperament and internalizing symptoms, Rabinowitz et al. (2016) found that behavioral withdrawal (an individual difference that overlaps with behavioral inhibition and negative emotional reactivity) was associated with internalizing symptoms for youth living in neighborhoods characterized by low social cohesion. Overall, these studies support the idea of a diathesis–stress model wherein temperament leaves some youth particularly vulnerable to risky contexts, but the number of studies is relatively few.

6 Contextual, Relational, and Dynamic Systems Theories

Frameworks that embody contextualism, such as bioecological systems theory (Bronfenbrenner & Morris, 2007), emphasize the dynamic influence of context on developmental outcomes. Contextualist theories posit that humans and human development can only be understood by examining the contexts and dynamic interactions within and between contexts in which we live and grow (Lerner et al., 2015). Increasingly, temperament research has adopted a contextualist framework, emphasizing that temperament develops in interactions of the child with the relationships, environment, and situations in which they find themselves. Moreover, temperament influences behaviors and outcomes via transactions between children's temperament and their broader developmental contexts (e.g., parental responses to their emotions and behaviors, family and classroom emotional climate, etc.). Importantly, contextual approaches have been helpful in identifying and unpacking individual differences and patterns of change in the development, expression, and outcomes associated with distinct facets of temperament.

Embedded within a bioecological systems model is the family system, which represents the earliest and most proximal level of influence on children's development. According to family systems theory (FST) (Bowen, 1966), the family itself is a complex social system (Kerr & Bowen, 1988), involving interactions among subsystems of relationships. As reviewed in this Element, temperament impacts these relationships, influencing how individuals navigate challenges and conflict, how they provide warmth and support, and family members' social, emotional, and behavioral responses. Family systems theory includes a focus on processes – development is itself a process that is multiply determined by distinct processes, connections, and interactions – and dynamic, evolving relationships within and across family subsystems. Concepts from FST can provide a framework for better understanding the role of temperament in other developmental contexts. Dynamic, relational systems theories can be applied to identify specific relationships that may influence temperament within and across the contexts children navigate, and can also provide detailed theoretical explanations for why and how certain emotional or relational dynamics in those relationships may interact to uniquely influence temperament phenotypically (e.g., how temperament or emotionality is manifesting), functionally (e.g., how different temperament manifestations may operate in different family environments), and developmentally (e.g., how the trajectory of temperament may change over time).

Similar to other developmental topics, temperament is primarily studied in Western, predominantly White European, heterosexual, and cisgender parent-led families. To date, less work has examined temperament in more diverse family settings, where relationships may be embedded in more dynamic, intersectional, or culturally rooted conceptions of child and family emotional functioning (e.g., societal "scripts" about emotionality and the appropriateness of discrete emotional expressions for both children and adults). Thus, there is an opportunity to examine the nature and developmental effects of culturally specific determinants of children's emotionality and self-regulation. Family systems theory has been used to understand more deeply cultural diversity and sociocultural determinants of family functioning, particularly around parental racial and ethnic socialization (e.g., James et al., 2018; Jones et al., 2021), but also gender socialization (e.g., Skinner & McHale, 2022), and their effects on child development. Additionally, FST devotes attention to how individuals (parents and children) are nested within complex, interconnected, interdependent, multidimensional family structures, which can guide scholars to more intentionally identify system-level variables that might influence child temperament and developmental outcomes, such as roles and expectations in co-parenting relationships, sibling relationships, child interactions with other relatives, and children's sense of emotional security and individuation within the family. Thus, because culture, identity, and nuanced contextual factors dynamically influence family structures and relationships, relational and dynamic systems theories may provide an avenue for temperament research to more strategically apply a multicultural and inclusive lens to studying temperament's development within and across diverse families.

7 Clinical and Translational Implications for Child Temperament

There are a number of ways that current temperament research has and can be incorporated into prevention and clinical intervention aimed at supporting children's healthy development. These include the development or implementation of early interventions that could alter children's temperamental trajectories and developmental outcomes, interventions centered on family dynamics and family-level factors, and interventions that target parents and more specific parent–child interactions.

Current temperament-based interventions are implemented in infancy and early childhood (e.g., Collings et al., 2017; McClowry & Collins, 2012) and often focus on caregiving (Iverson & Gartstein, 2018) or aim to identify and address which elements of temperament may operate as risk or protective factors against childhood behavior or psychological problems (Schwebel & Plumert, 1999). Incorporating a family systems perspective may offer practical support for these efforts and assist in identifying (and subsequently targeting) specific family-level disruptions, such as particular family processes that might alter the development of children's temperament toward a risky trajectory. Addressing dysfunctional and maladaptive family processes early on and substituting them with more adaptive relational strategies may positively influence the development of temperament and prevent the manifestation of early emotional, behavioral, or social problems.

Relatedly, providing parents, caregivers, and educators with an understanding of temperament can validate their experiences of children when they present challenging temperament-related behaviors, while also enhancing their perspective, attitudes, and empathy toward children's individual differences. Behavioral parenting interventions can be improved by taking children's individual differences in threat and reward sensitivity, impulsivity, effortful control, and emotion regulation into account, providing parents and caregivers with specific strategies and practices to be more effective with children's temperament characteristics in mind. McClowry's (McClowry & Collins, 2012) school-based intervention supports children's understanding of temperament and provides emotion and self-regulation skills. This program can also provide educators with information about temperament and how it impacts learning and classroom behaviors, as well as tools for more effectively supporting children's academic, social, emotional, and behavioral competencies.

Similarly, individual treatments with older children and adolescents can incorporate information about temperament to support better understanding of the contribution of temperament to their emotional and behavioral problems. Treatment can be tailored to provide tools and skills specific to managing children's emotionality and impulsivity and building their self-regulation, similar to the way that dialectical behavior therapy provides tools and support in these areas (Linehan, 2014). Incorporating temperament in clinical settings may also aid clinical case conceptualizations of adverse emotional and behavioral outcomes presented by parents and children. Thus, reductions in behavioral challenges associated with temperament may yield higher-order benefits downstream for youth and parental functioning, interparental or co-parenting functioning, and broader family-level functioning that could promote resilience and well-being for all family members (Allmann et al., 2016). Dynamic relational and systems approaches can be used to identify, understand, and build or support resilience or promotive processes within families featuring diverse compositions, structures, and backgrounds, tapping into culturally rooted or culturally informed communication styles and relational dimensions that support resilience and family well-being (Panter-Brick, 2015; Spencer et al., 2019).

8 Future Directions in Research and Practice

Our understanding of temperament – its neurobiological roots, how it develops and changes over time, and how it influences developmental outcomes – has grown and evolved over several decades, and there continues to be opportunities to challenge and advance research on temperament by integrating developmental, transactional, and contextual approaches more comprehensively. Importantly, future research could address the question of how temperament operates or functions within and across distinct, diverse developmental contexts by incorporating systems and relational theories to study temperament in more nuanced, integrative, and multifaceted ways.

Critical to addressing such questions is a deeper understanding of construct measurement and validity. Prior seminal reviews have discussed the relative strengths and weaknesses of using questionnaire and observational measures (e.g., Rothbart & Bates, 2007). For example, questionnaire measures offer reporters' perspectives over time and across situations, whereas observational measures can provide more precise assessments of individual differences in the characteristic being assessed, and physiological measures are relatively free of reporter or observer biases. However, observational and physiological assessments offer only brief samples, often in a setting that is not ecologically valid. Despite increased understanding of neurobiological underpinnings of temperament and delineation of expected emotional and behavioral responses to specific stimuli, our understanding of correspondence or lack of correspondence among different measurement methods has not advanced. Research is needed that facilitates understanding of how, when, and for whom physiological activation translates into observable behaviors in particular situations, and how those translate into parents', teachers', children's, and researchers' observations of those behaviors.

Along similar lines, a more nuanced understanding of how temperament is related to developmental outcomes might be achieved when multiple temperament dimensions or characteristics are examined simultaneously, particularly in examining reactivity-by-regulation interactions or capturing the simultaneous contributions of multiple characteristics in person-oriented or profile approaches (e.g., Moran et al., 2017). To date, studies have examined interactions between one emotional reactivity variable and one regulation variable. It is likely that these interactions are complex, with multiple emotionality and self-regulation variables simultaneously at play. Studies with sufficient power to examine complex interactions or person-centered analytic approaches that allow the consideration of several characteristics at once are needed.

There is now a substantive literature demonstrating impressive growth and growth-related implications of temperament with respect to outcomes (e.g., symptoms, disorders), especially in early childhood. What is lacking is an integration of different domains of developmental growth. That is, temperament does not develop "in a vacuum," and there are important connections with other areas of development – physical maturation and cognitive advances in particular. For example, rapid increases in fearfulness at the end of the first year of life have been attributed in part to advances in locomotor abilities and the fact that infants who are able to crawl or scoot encounter more dangerous objects and situations, making increases in fear and avoidance adaptive. One study suggested that the experience of crawling could generate and refine functions required for the onset of "wariness of heights," and other forms of fearfulness may also be implicated. This work with the visual cliff has also pointed to individual differences, with some infants approaching rather than avoiding what appears to be a drop, despite all infants experiencing physiological arousal (Ueno et al., 2012). Gains in fear expression could also be a product of improvements in memory, enabling infants to readily detect novelty in their surroundings. Empirical studies examining these connections across physical, cognitive, and emotional maturation are needed.

There is a similar need to examine temperament in relation to puberty-related physiological, cognitive, emotional, and social changes in adolescence. Similar to infancy, adolescence is a developmental period marked by rapid and substantial growth. However, with notable exceptions (e.g., Lawson et al., 2022), temperament development has not been studied extensively in a manner that enables us to consider trajectories and underlying processes, modeling antecedents and consequences of the changes. A variety of models linking temperament and psychopathology have been proposed and require a closer examination across different developmental periods. That is, a vulnerability model may best describe a connection of fearfulness or behavioral inhibition with anxiety in early childhood, but in adolescence related effects are likely different, with the social and contextual implications of social anxiety, for example, potentially shaping temperament. Overall, more research is needed spanning developmental periods to better understand the potential of changing roles of temperament over time.

Integrating temperament research with research on other developmental processes will also facilitate a better understanding of the processes at play in the effects of temperament on children's developmental outcomes. A fair amount of research examines the interplay between temperament and parenting in relation to children's social, emotional, and behavioral adjustment (Kiff et al., 2011), but there is less research examining other family, peer, and teacher relationships, and factors in community and neighborhood contexts that might mediate or moderate temperament-adjustment associations and that might interact with parenting influences. In addition, little research has examined intrapersonal cognitive-behavioral mechanisms of the effects of temperament on adjustment; and increased attention to variables such as attributional biases, appraisal, coping, and other emotion-regulation strategies is needed.

Furthermore, it is critical that research examining temperament, parenting, and family relationships does so in samples representing diverse family structures and social, cultural, and socioeconomic experiences, especially in non-Western countries, to more accurately estimate the magnitude of temperament effects, better characterize how temperament might operate differently in these varied contexts, and examine potential moderators serving as protective factors in different contexts. To that end, temperament research can also employ relational and dynamic systems theory. Clear evidence points to the complex effects of temperament on family relationships, as family subsystems influence and interact with each other. Nonetheless, a better understanding of the contexts, magnitudes, and extent of these effects is needed. Future research should examine multiple family subsystems simultaneously, account for the effects of contextual factors, and examine temperament, personality, and family relationships across cultures. In addition, it will be valuable to understand how sociocultural changes (e.g., the COVID-19 pandemic, wars and political conflicts, shifts in one-child-per-family policy in China, or social/digital media use) shape temperament development or might have varied effects on children's developmental outcomes based on temperament.

Finally, considerations of incorporating temperament in prevention and clinical interventions are intriguing, but it is critical to evaluate whether doing so enhances intervention effectiveness. In addition, temperament-based interventions require further evaluation, explicitly examining potential moderators (e.g., parental level of education, experiences of stress or adversity) as well as mediators (e.g., changes in parent–child or teacher–child interactions, increases in effective emotion-regulation strategies) of their effects. This, additionally, would enhance our understanding of the etiological role temperament plays in children's developmental outcomes.

9 Conclusions

Child temperament is a complex construct influenced by myriad factors, including genetics, biology, family relationships and dynamics, as well as broader social and cultural factors. Current research offers a number of important conclusions, also demonstrating that a fuller understanding of children's temperament and its contribution to their developmental outcomes requires us to capture the complex interplay of temperament with social and contextual influences, considering integrated developmental, transactional, and relational models. Simultaneously, delineating the contribution of contextual factors to children's development requires consideration of how children's temperament differentiates the impact of social and contextual factors on their development.

Since Rothbart and Bates' (1998) comprehensive review of the role of temperament in children's development, temperament research has advanced in several ways. The research reviewed here elaborates the field's enhanced understanding of neurobiological systems underlying temperament behaviors, which has advanced our ability to link biological markers with behavioral manifestations of temperament. Research has also expanded evidence of the role of temperament in contributing to developmental outcomes other than psychopathology, including social–emotional and academic competencies and health behaviors. The field has increasingly elaborated how temperament operates in relation to other variables, with greater attention to examining the effects of temperament within the contexts of parenting and family, school, peer, and neighborhood relationships, and considering broader sociocultural and economic factors.

While there is substantial evidence of bidirectional effects of temperament and parenting throughout childhood, the field has also provided an expanded understanding of experiences that shape temperament and its increased role in transactions and interactions with parents, other family members, teachers, and peers in middle childhood and preadolescence. By adolescence, as youth gain greater independence in selecting and engaging in different relationships and contexts, these effects appear to become more direct, independent, and evocative.

Finally, the research reviewed here highlights how temperament characteristics can shape development by altering the direction, exposure to, and strength of other influences, directly and indirectly through evocative and moderating effects. By incorporating contextual, relational, and dynamic systems theories, researchers and clinicians can gain a deeper understanding of how family relationships, emotional climate, and role expectations shape and are shaped by a child's temperament, and how these might differ in varying cultural and social contexts. Ultimately, an integrated approach that incorporates individual, familial, and contextual factors – and examines the interrelations within and among these different factors, in both form and function – will provide a more comprehensive understanding of child temperament and its implications for child development and well-being.

References

Abitante, G., Haraden, D. A., Pine, A., Cole, D., & Garber, J. (2022). Trajectories of positive and negative affect across adolescence: Maternal history of depression and adolescent sex as predictors. *Journal of Affective Disorders, 315*, 96–104. https://doi.org/10.1016/j.jad.2022.07.038.

Acar, I. H., Rudasill, K. M., Molfese, V., Torquati, J., & Prokasky, A. (2015). Temperament and preschool children's peer interactions. *Early Education and Development, 26*(4), 479–495. https://doi.org/10.1080/10409289.2015.1000718.

Ackerman, B. P., Brown, E. D., & Izard, C. E. (2004). The relations between persistent poverty and contextual risk and children's behavior in elementary school. *Developmental Psychology, 40*(3), 367–377. https://doi.org/10.1037/0012-1649.40.3.367.

Ainsworth, M. S. (1979). Infant–mother attachment. *American Psychologist, 34*(10), 932–937. https://doi.org/10.1037/0003-066X.34.10.932.

Allen, J. P., & Loeb, E. L. (2015). The autonomy-connection challenge in adolescent–peer relationships. *Child Development Perspectives, 9*(2), 101–105. https://doi.org/10.1111/cdep.12111.

Allmann, A. E., Kopala-Sibley, D. C., & Klein, D. N. (2016). Preschoolers' psychopathology and temperament predict mothers' later mood disorders. *Journal of Abnormal Child Psychology, 44*, 421–432. https://doi.org/10.1007/s10802-015-0058-z.

Almy, B., Kuskowski, M., Malone, S. M., Myers, E., & Luciana, M. (2018). A longitudinal analysis of adolescent decision-making with the Iowa Gambling Task. *Developmental Psychology, 54*(4), 689–702. https://doi.org/10.1037/dev0000460.

Alvik, A., Torgersen, A. M., Aalen, O. O., & Lindemann, R. (2011). Binge alcohol exposure once a week in early pregnancy predicts temperament and sleeping problems in the infant. *Early Human Development, 87*, 827–833. https://doi.org/10.1016/j.earlhumdev.2011.06.009.

Andreas, J. B., & Watson, M. W. (2016). Person–environment interactions and adolescent substance use: The role of sensation seeking and perceived neighborhood risk. *Journal of Child & Adolescent Substance Abuse, 25*(5), 438–447. https://doi.org/10.1080/1067828X.2015.1066722.

Antonelli, M. C., Pallares, M. E., Ceccatelli, S., & Spulber, S. (2016). Long-term consequences of prenatal stress and neurotoxicants exposure on neurodevelopment. *Progress in Neurobiology, 155*, 21–35. https://doi.org/10.1016/j.pneurobio.2016.05.005.

Araiza, A. M., Freitas, A. L., & Klein, D. N. (2020). Social-experience and temperamental predictors of rejection sensitivity: A prospective study. *Social Psychological and Personality Science, 11*(6), 733–742. https://doi.org/10.1177/1948550619878422.

Arcus, D. (2001). Inhibited and uninhibited children: Biology in the social context. In T. D. Wachs, R. R. McCrae, & G. A. Kohnstamm (Eds.), *Temperament in context*, 1st ed. (pp. 43–60). New York: Psychology Press. https://doi.org/10.4324/9781410600967.

Atherton, O. E., Zheng, L. R., Bleidorn, W., & Robins, R. W. (2019). The codevelopment of effortful control and school behavioral problems. *Journal of Personality and Social Psychology, 117*(3), 659–673. https://doi.org/10.1037/pspp0000201.

Ato, E., Galián, M. D., & Fernández-Vilar, M. A. (2015). The moderating role of children's effortful control in the relation between marital adjustment and parenting. *Journal of Child and Family Studies, 24*(11), 3341–3349. https://doi.org/10.1007/s10826-015-0136-4.

Ato, E., Fernández-Vilar, M. Á., & Galián, M. D. (2020). Relation between temperament and school adjustment in Spanish children: A person-centered approach. *Frontiers in Psychology, 11*, 250. https://doi.org/10.3389/fpsyg.2020.00250.

Australian Institute of Family Studies. (2015). The longitudinal study of Australian children: Data user guide – November 2015. Melbourne.

Baardstu, S., Coplan, R. J., Karevold, E. B., Laceulle, O. M., & von Soest, T. (2020). Longitudinal pathways from shyness in early childhood to personality in adolescence: Do peers matter? *Journal of Research on Adolescence, 30*, 362–379. https://doi.org/10.1111/jora.12482.

Balle, M., Fiol-Veny, A., de la Torre-Luque, A., Llabres, J., & Bornas, X. (2022). Temperamental change in adolescence and its predictive role on anxious symptomatology. *Behavioral Sciences, 12*(6), 194. https://doi.org/10.3390/bs12060194.

Barker, E. D., Jaffee, S. R., Uher, R., & Maughan, B. (2011). The contribution of prenatal and postnatal maternal anxiety and depression to child maladjustment. *Depression and Anxiety, 28*(8), 696–702. https://doi.org/10.1002/da.20856.

Bates, J. E., & Pettit, G. S. (2007). Temperament, parenting, and socialization. In J. E. Grusec & P. D. Hastings (Eds.), *Handbook of socialization: Theory and research* (pp. 153–177). New York: Guilford Press.

Bates, J. E., Schermerhorn, A. C., & Petersen, I. T. (2012). Temperament and parenting in developmental perspective. In M. Zentner & R. Shiner (Eds.), *The handbook of temperament* (pp. 425–441). New York: Guilford Press.

Bates, J. E., Schermerhorn, A. C., & Petersen, I. T. (2014). Temperament concepts in developmental psychopathology. In M. Lewis & K. D. Rudolph (Eds.), *Handbook of developmental psychopathology* (pp. 311–329). New York: Springer.

Bates, R. A., Singletary, B., Dynia, J. M., & Justice, L. M. (2021). Temperament and sleep behaviors in infants and toddlers living in low-income homes. *Infant Behavior and Development*, *65*, 101657. https://doi.org/10.1016/j.infbeh.2021.101657.

Bayly, B., & Gartstein, M. (2013). Mother's and father's reports on their child's temperament: Does gender matter? *Infant Behavior and Development*, *36*, 171–175. https://doi.org/10.1016/j.infbeh.2012.10.008.

Beauchaine T. P. (2015). Respiratory sinus arrhythmia: A transdiagnostic biomarker of emotion dysregulation and psychopathology. *Current Opinion in Psychology*, *3*, 43–47. https://doi.org/10.1016/j.copsyc.2015.01.017.

Beceren, B. Ö., & Özdemir, A. A. (2019). Role of temperament traits and empathy skills of preschool children in predicting emotional adjustment. *International Journal of Progressive Education*, *15*(3), 91–107. https://hdl.handle.net/11499/28385.

Behrendt, H. F., Wade, M., Bayet, L., Nelson, C. A., & Enlow, M. B. (2020). Pathways to social–emotional functioning in the preschool period: The role of child temperament and maternal anxiety in boys and girls. *Development and Psychopathology*, *32*(3), 961–974. https://doi.org/10.1017/S0954579419000853.

Bengtsson, H., Arvidsson, Å., & Nyström, B. (2022). Negative emotionality and peer status: Evidence for bidirectional longitudinal influences during the elementary school years. *School Psychology International*, *43*(1), 88–105. https://doi.org/10.1177/01430343211063546.

Bernier, A., Calkins, S. D., & Bell, M. A. (2016) Longitudinal associations between the quality of mother–infant interactions and brain development across infancy. *Child Development*, *87*, 1159–1174. https://doi.org/10.1111/cdev.12518.

Blair, C., Granger, D. A., Willoughby, M., Mills-Koonce, R., Cox, M., Greenberg, M. T., Kivlighan, K. T., Fortunato, C. K., & FLP Investigators (2011). Salivary cortisol mediates effects of poverty and parenting on executive functions in early childhood. *Child Development*, *82*(6), 1970–1984. https://doi.org/10.1111/j.1467-8624.2011.01643.x.

Blankson, A. N., O'Brien, M., Leerkes, E. M., Marcovitch, S., & Calkins, S. D. (2011). Shyness and vocabulary: The roles of executive functioning and home environmental stimulation. *Merrill-Palmer Quarterly*, *57*, 105–128. https://doi.org/10.1353/mpq.2011.0007.

Border, R., Johnson, E. C., Evans, L. M., Smolen, A., Berley, N., Sullivan, P. F., & Keller, M. C. (2019). No support for historical candidate gene or candidate gene-by-interaction hypotheses for major depression across multiple large samples. *American Journal of Psychiatry, 176*(5), 376–387. https://doi.org/10.1176/appi.ajp.2018.18070881.

Bornstein, M. H. (2017). The specificity principle in acculturation science. *Perspectives on Psychological Science, 12*(1), 3–45. https://doi.org/10.1177/1745691616655997.

Bornstein, M. H., & Cote. L. R. (2009). Child temperament in three U.S. cultural groups. *Infant Mental Health Journal, 30*, 433–451. https://doi.org/10.1002/imhj.20223.

Bornstein, M. H., Putnick, D. L., & Esposito, G. (2017). Continuity and stability in development. *Child Development Perspectives, 11*, 113–119. https://doi.org/10.1111/cdep.12221.

Bornstein, M. H., Hahn, C.-S., Putnick, D., & Pearson, R. (2019). Stability of child temperament: Multiple moderation by child and mother characteristics. *British Journal of Developmental Psychology, 37*, 51–67. https://doi.org/10.1111/bjdp.12253.

Bowen, M. (1966). The use of family theory in clinical practice. *Comprehensive Psychiatry, 7*(5), 345–374. https://doi.org/10.1017/S0954579419000488.

Boyce, W. T., & Ellis, B. J. (2005). Biological sensitivity to context: I. An evolutionary-developmental theory of the origins and functions of stress reactivity. *Developmental Psychopathology, 17*, 271–301. https://doi.org/10.1017/S0954579405050145.

Branje, S. (2018). Development of parent–adolescent relationships: Conflict interactions as a mechanism of change. *Child Development Perspectives, 12* (3), 171–176. https://doi.org/10.1111/cdep.12278.

Braungart-Rieker, J. M., Hill-Soderlund, A. L., & Karrass, J. (2010). Fear and anger reactivity trajectories from 4 to 16 months: The roles of temperament, regulation, and maternal sensitivity. *Developmental Psychology, 46*, 791–804. https://doi.org/10.1037/a0019673.

Brendgen, M., Wanner, B., Morin, A. J., & Vitaro, F. (2005). Relations with parents and with peers, temperament, and trajectories of depressed mood during early adolescence. *Journal of Abnormal Child Psychology, 33*(5), 579–594. https://doi.org/10.1007/s10802-005-6739-2.

Bridgett, D. J., Gartstein, M. A., Putnam, S. P., McKay, T., Iddins, E., Robertson, C., . . . & Rittmueller, A. (2009). Maternal and contextual influences and the effect of temperament development during infancy on parenting in toddlerhood. *Infant Behavior and Development, 32*(1), 103–116. https://doi.org/10.1016/j.infbeh.2008.10.007.

Bridgett, D. J., Laake, L. M., Gartstein, M. A., & Dorn, D. (2013). Development of infant positive emotionality: The contribution of maternal characteristics and effects on subsequent parenting. *Infant and Child Development*, *22*(4), 362–382. https://doi.org/10.1002/icd.1795.

Bridgett, D. J., Burt, N. M., Edwards, E. S., & Deater-Deckard, K. (2015). Intergenerational transmission of self-regulation: A multidisciplinary review and integrative conceptual framework. *Psychological Bulletin*, *141*(3), 602. https://doi.org/10.1037/a0038662.

Brody, G. H., Stoneman, Z., & McCoy, J. K. (1994). Forecasting sibling relationships in early adolescence from child temperaments and family processes in middle childhood. *Child Development*, *65*(3), 771–784. https://doi.org/10.1111/j.1467-8624.1994.tb00782.x.

Brody G. H., Yu, R., Miller, G. E., & Chen, E. (2023). Longitudinal links between early adolescent temperament and inflammation among young black adults. *Psychoneuroendocrinology*, *152*, 106077. https://doi.org/10.1016/j.psyneuen.2023.106077.

Broekhuizen, M. L., van Aken, M. A. G., Dubas, J. S., Mulder, H., & Leseman, P. P. M. (2015). Individual differences in effects of child care quality: The role of child affective self-regulation and gender. *Infant Behavior and Development*, *40*, 216–230. https://doi.org/10.1016/j.infbeh.2015.06.009.

Bronfenbrenner, U., & Morris, P. A. (2007). The bioecological model of human development. In R. M. Lerner & W. Damon (Eds.), *Handbook of child psychology, vol. 1: Theoretical models of human development*, 6th ed. (pp. 793–828). Hoboken, NJ: Wiley.

Bruce, J., Fisher, P. A., Pears, K. C., & Levine, S. (2009). Morning cortisol levels in preschool-aged foster children: Differential effects of maltreatment type. *Developmental Psychobiology: Journal of the International Society for Developmental Psychobiology*, *51*(1), 14–23. https://doi.org/10.1002/dev.20333.

Brumariu, L. E., & Kerns, K. A. (2013). Pathways to anxiety: Contributions of attachment history, temperament, peer competence, and ability to manage intense emotions. *Child Psychiatry & Human Development*, *44*, 504–515. https://doi.org/10.1007/s10578-012-0345-7.

Burton, P., Wells, J. C. K., Kennedy, K., Nicholl, R., Khakoo, A., & Fewtrell, M. S. (2011). Association between infant correlates of impulsivity – surgency (extraversion) – and early infant growth. *Appetite*, *57*, 504–509. https://doi.org/10.1016/j.appet.2011.07.002.

Bush, N. R., Lengua, L. J., & Colder, C. R. (2010). Temperament as a moderator of the relation between neighborhood and children's adjustment. *Journal of Applied Developmental Psychology*, *31*(5), 351–361. https://doi.org/10.1016/j.appdev.2010.06.004.

Bush, N. R., Jones-Mason, K., Coccia, M., Caron, Z., Alkon, A., Thomas, M., ...
& Epel, E. (2017). Effects of pre-and postnatal maternal stress on infant
temperament and autonomic nervous system reactivity and regulation in
a diverse, low-income population. *Development and Psychopathology, 29*,
1553–1571. https://doi.org/10.1017/S0954579417001237.

Buss, A. H., & Plomin, R. (1975). *A temperament theory of personality development.* New York: Wiley-Interscience.

Buss, K. A., & Kiel, E. J. (2011). Do maternal protective behaviors alleviate
toddlers' fearful distress? *Infant Behavior and Development, 35*, 136–143.
https://doi.org/10.1177/0165025410375922.

Buss, K. A., & Kiel, A. J. (2013). Temperamental risk factors for pediatric
anxiety disorders. In R. A. Vasa & A. K. Roy (Eds.), *Pediatric anxiety
disorders: A clinical guide* (pp. 47–68). New York: Springer Science and
Business Media. https://doi.org/10.1007/978-1-4614-6599-7_3.

Buss, K. A., Dennis, T. A., Brooker, R. J., & Sippel, L. M. (2011). An ERP study
of conflict monitoring in 4–8-year old children: Associations with temperament. *Developmental Cognitive Neuroscience, 1*(2), 131–140. https://doi
.org/10.1016/j.dcn.2010.12.003

Buss, K. A., Zhou, A. M., & Trainer, A. (2021). Bidirectional effects of toddler
temperament and maternal overprotection on maternal and child anxiety
symptoms across preschool. *Depression and Anxiety, 38*(12), 1201–1210.
https://doi.org/10.1002/da.23199.

Calkins, S. D., & Fox, N. A. (1992). The relations among infant temperament,
security of attachment, and behavioral inhibition at twenty-four months. *Child
Development, 63*(6), 1456–1472. https://doi.org/10.1111/j.1467-8624.1992
.tb01707.x.

Calkins, S. D., Fox, N. A., & Marshall, T. R. (1996). Behavioral and physiological antecedents of inhibited and uninhibited behavior. *Child
Development, 67*, 523–540. https://doi.org/10.2307/1131830.

Campos, J. J., Bertenthal, B. I., & Kermoian, R. (1992). Early experience and
emotional development: The emergence of wariness of heights.
Psychological Science, 3, 61–64. https://doi.org/10.1111/j.1467-9280.1992
.tb00259.x.

Carey, W. B. (1985). Temperament and increased weight gain in infants.
Developmental Behavioral Pediatrics, 6, 128–131.

Carlson, S. M., Davis, A. C., & Leach, J. G. (2005). Less is more: Executive
function and symbolic representation in preschool children. *Psychological
Science, 16*(8), 609–616. https://doi.org/10.1111/j.1467-9280.2005.01583.x.

Carranza, J. A., Pérez-López, J., Salinas, M. D. C. G., & Martínez-Fuentes,
M. T. (2000). A longitudinal study of temperament in infancy: Stability and

convergence of measures. *European Journal of Personality*, *14*, 21–37. doi:10.1002/(sici)1099-0984(200001/02)14:1.

Carson, D. K., & Bittner, M. T. (1994). Temperament and school-aged children's coping abilities and responses to stress. *Journal of Genetic Psychology*, *155*(3), 289–302. https://doi.org/10.1080/00221325.1994.9914779.

Caspi, A., & Shiner, R. (2008). Temperament and personality. *Rutter's Child and Adolescent Psychiatry*, 182–198. https://doi.org/10.1002/978144 4300895.

Caspi, A., Roberts, B. W., & Shiner, R. L. (2005). Personality development: Stability and change. *Annual Review of Psychology*, *56*, 453–484. https://doi .org/10.1146/annurev.psych.55.090902.141913.

Cassidy, J., Woodhouse, S. S., Sherman, L. J., Stupica, B., & Lejuez, C. W. (2011). Enhancing infant attachment security: An examination of treatment efficacy and differential susceptibility. *Development and Psychopathology*, *23*(1), 131–148. https://doi.org/10.1017/S0954579410000696.

Cerniglia, L., Cimino, S., & Ballarotto, G. (2014). Mother–child and father–child interaction with their 24-month-old children during feeding, considering paternal involvement and the child's temperament in a community sample. *Infant Mental Health Journal*, *35*(5), 473–481. https://doi.org/ 10.1002/imhj.21466.

Chang, H., Shelleby, E. C., Cheong, J., & Shaw, D. S. (2012). Cumulative risk, negative emotionality, and emotion regulation as predictors of social competence in transition to school: A mediated moderation model. *Social Development*, *21*(4), 780–800. https://doi.org/10.1111/j.1467-9507.2011 .00648.x.

Chen, X. (2018). Culture, temperament, and social and psychological adjustment. *Developmental Review*, *50*, 42–53. https://doi.org/10.1016/ j.dr.2018.03.004.

Chen, X., Hastings, P. D., Rubin, K. H., Chen, H., Cen, G., & Stewart, S. L. (1998). Child-rearing attitudes and behavioral inhibition in Chinese and Canadian toddlers: A cross-cultural study. *Developmental psychology*, *34*, 677. https://doi.org/10.1037/0012-1649.34.4.677.

Chen, X., Rubin, K. H., Liu, M., Chen, H., Wang, L., Li, D., . . . & Li, B. (2003). Compliance in Chinese and Canadian toddlers: A cross-cultural study. *International Journal of Behavioral Development*, *27*, 428–436. https://doi .org/10.1080/01650250344000046.

Chess, S., & Thomas, A. (1991). Temperament and the concept of goodness of fit. In J. Strelau & A. Angleitner (Eds.), *Explorations in temperament: International perspectives on theory and measurement* (pp. 15–28). New York: Plenum Press.

Clark, D. A., Durbin, C. E., Heitzeg, M. M., Iacono, W. G., McGue, M., & Hicks, B. M. (2023). Personality and peer groups in adolescence: Reciprocal associations and shared genetic and environmental influences. *Journal of Personality, 91*(2), 464–481. https://doi.org/10.1111/jopy.12741.

Coan, J. A., & Allen, J. J. B. (2004). Frontal EEG asymmetry as a moderator and mediator of emotion. *Biological Psychology, 67*, 7–49. https://doi.org/10.1016/j.biopsycho.2004.03.002.

Colder, C. R., & O'Connor, R. M. (2004). Gray's reinforcement sensitivity model and child psychopathology: Laboratory and questionnaire assessment of the BAS and BIS. *Journal of Abnormal Child Psychology, 32*, 435–451. https://doi.org/10.1023/B:JACP.0000030296.54122.b6.

Colder, C. R., Hawk, L. W. Jr., Lengua, L. J., Wiezcorek, W. F., Eiden, R. D., Read, J. P. (2013). Trajectories of reinforcement sensitivity during adolescence and risk for substance use. *Journal of Research on Adolescence, 23*(2), 345–356. https://doi.org/10.1111/jora.12001.

Collings, A., O'Connor, E., & McClowry, S. (2017). The role of a temperament intervention in kindergarten children's standardized academic achievement. *Journal of Education and Training Studies, 5*(2), 120–139.

Compas, B. E., Connor-Smith, J. K., Saltzman, H., Thomsen, A. H., & Wadsworth, M. E. (2001). Coping with stress during childhood and adolescence: Problems, progress, and potential in theory and research. *Psychological Bulletin, 127*(1), 87. https://doi.org/10.1037/0033-2909.127.1.87.

Compas, B. E., Connor-Smith, J., & Jaser, S. S. (2004). Temperament, stress reactivity, and coping: Implications for depression in childhood and adolescence. *Journal of Clinical Child and Adolescent Psychology, 33*(1), 21–31. https://doi.org/10.1207/S15374424JCCP3301_3.

Conger, R. D., Ge, X., Elder, G. H. Jr., Lorenz, F. O., & Simons, R. L. (1994). Economic stress, coercive family process, and developmental problems of adolescents. *Child Development, 65*(2), 541–561. https://doi.org/10.1111/j.1467-8624.1994.tb00768.x.

Conger, R. D., Wallace, L. E., Sun, Y., Simons, R. L., McLoyd, V. C., & Brody, G. H. (2002). Economic pressure in African American families: A replication and extension of the family stress model. *Developmental Psychology, 38*(2), 179. https://doi.org/10.1037/0012-1649.38.2.179.

Corapci, F. (2004). Cumulative and interactive influences of risk and protective factors upon social competence of low-income preschool children. ETD Collection for Purdue University.

Corapci, F. (2008). The role of child temperament on Head Start preschoolers' social competence in the context of cumulative risk. *Journal of Applied*

Developmental Psychology, *29*(1), 1–16. https://doi.org/10.1016/j.appdev .2007.10.003.

Creemers, H. E., Dijkstra, J. K., Vollebergh, W. A., Ormel, J., Verhulst, F. C., & Huizink, A. C. (2010). Predicting life-time and regular cannabis use during adolescence; the roles of temperament and peer substance use: the TRAILS study. *Addiction*, *105*(4), 699–708. https://doi.org/10.1111/j.1360-0443 .2009.02819.x.

Crockenberg, S. C., & Leerkes, E. M. (2006). Infant and maternal behavior moderate reactivity to novelty to predict anxious behavior at 2.5 years. *Development and Psychopathology*, *18*, 17–34. https://doi.org/10.1037/0012-1649 .40.6.1123.

Cross-Disorder Group of the Psychiatric Genomics Consortium. (2019). Genomic relationships, novel loci, and pleiotropic mechanisms across eight psychiatric disorders. *Cell*, *179*(7), 1469–1482. https://doi.org/10.1016/ j.cell.2019.11.020.

Darlington, A. E., & Wright, C. M. (2006). The influence of temperament on weight gain in early infancy. *Journal of Developmental and Behavioral Pediatrics*, *27*(4), 329–335.

Davis, E. P., Glynn, L. M., Dunkel Schetter, C., Hobel, C., Chicz-DeMet, A., & Sandman, C. A. (2007). Prenatal exposure to maternal depression and cortisol influences infant temperament. *Journal of the American Academy of Child & Adolescent Psychiatry*, *46*, 737–746. https://doi.org/10.1097/ chi.0b013e318047b775.

Dawe, S., Gullo M. J., Loxton N. J. (2004). Reward drive and rash impulsiveness as dimensions of impulsivity: Implications for substance misuse. *Addictive Behaviors*, *29*(7), 1389–1405. https://doi.org/10.1016/j.addbeh.2004.06.004.

De Bolle, M., Beyers, W., De Clercq, B., & De Fruyt, F. (2012). General personality and psychopathology in referred and nonreferred children and adolescents: An investigation of continuity, pathoplasty, and complication models. *Journal of Abnormal Psychology*, *121*(4), 958–970. https://doi.org/ 10.1037/a0027742.

de la Torre-Luque, A., Fiol-Veny, A., Balle, M., Nelemans, S. A., & Bornas, X. (2020). Anxiety in early adolescence: Heterogeneous developmental trajectories, associations with risk factors and depressive symptoms. *Child Psychiatry and Human Development*, *51*, 527–541. https://doi.org/10.1007/ s10578-019-00936-y.

de Maat, D. A., Schuurmans, I. K., Jongerling, J., Metcalf, S. A., Lucassen, N., Franken, I. H., … & Jansen, P. W. (2022). Early life stress and behavior problems in early childhood: Investigating the contributions of child temperament and executive functions to resilience. *Child Development,* *93*(1), e1–e16. https://doi.org/10.1111/cdev.13663.

De Pauw, S. S. W. (2016). Childhood personality and temperament. In T. Widiger (Ed.), *The Oxford handbook of the five-factor-model of personality* (pp. 243–280). New York: Oxford University Press.

de Rooij, S. R., Painter, R. C., Phillips, D. I., Raikkonen, K., Schene, A. H., & Roseboom, T. J. (2011). Self-reported depression and anxiety after prenatal famine exposure: Mediation by cardio-metabolic pathology? *Journal of Developmental Origins of Health and Disease, 2,* 136–143. https://doi.org/ 10.1017/S2040174411000055.

Depue, R. A., & Collins, P. F. (1999). Neurobiology of the structure of personality: Dopamine, facilitation of incentive motivation, and extraversion. *Behavioral Brain Science, 22,* 491–517. https://doi.org/10.1017/S0140525 X99002046.

Dich, N., Doan, S. N., & Evans, G. W. (2017). In risky environments, emotional children have more behavioral problems but lower allostatic load. *Health Psychology, 36*(5), 468–476. https://doi.org/10.1037/hea0000459.

Dolcini-Catania, L. G., Byrne, M. L., Whittle, S., Schwartz, O., Simmons, J. G., & Allen, N. B. (2020). Temperament and symptom pathways to the development of adolescent depression. *Journal of Abnormal Child Psychology, 48* (6), 839–849. https://doi.org/10.1007/s10802-020-00638-3.

Dollar, J. M., & Stifter, C. A. (2012). Temperamental surgency and emotion regulation as predictors of childhood social competence. *Journal of Experimental Child Psychology, 112*(2), 178–194. https://doi.org/10.1016/ j.jecp.2012.02.004.

Dollar, J. M., Perry, N. B., Calkins, S. D., Keane, S. P., & Shanahan, L. (2018). Temperamental anger and positive reactivity and the development of social skills: Implications for academic competence during preadolescence. *Early Education and Development, 29*(5), 747–761.

Dougherty, L. R., Klein, D. N., Olino, T. M., Dyson, M., & Rose, S. (2009). Increased waking salivary cortisol and depression risk in preschoolers: The role of maternal history of melancholic depression and early child temperament. *Journal of Child Psychology and Psychiatry, 50,* 1495–1503. https://doi.org/10.1111/j.1469-7610.2009.02116.x.

Dougherty, L. R., Klein, D. N., Durbin, C. E., Hayden, E. P., & Olino, T. M. (2010). Temperamental positive and negative emotionality and children's depressive symptoms: A longitudinal prospective study from age three to age ten. *Journal of Social and Clinical Psychology, 29*(4), 462–488. https://doi .org/10.1521/jscp.2010.29.4.462.

Doussard-Roosevelt, J. A., Porges, S. W., Scanlon, J. W., Alemi, B., & Scanlon, K. B. (1997). Vagal regulation of heart rate in the prediction of developmental outcome for very low birth weight preterm infants. *Child Development, 68,* 173–186. https://doi.org/10.1111/j.1467-8624.1997.tb01934.x.

Dowd, J. B., Simanek, A. M., & Aiello, A. E. (2009). Socio-economic status, cortisol, and allostatic load: A review of the literature. *International Journal of Epidemiology, 38,* 1297–1309. https://doi.org/10.1093/ije/dyp277.

Dunn, J., Deater-Deckard, K., Pickering, K., & Golding, J. (1999). Siblings, parents, and partners: Family relationships within a longitudinal community study. *Journal of Child Psychology and Psychiatry, 40*(7), 1025–1037. https://doi.org/10.1111/1469-7610.00521.

Eggum-Wilkens, N. D., Reichenberg, R. E., Eisenberg, N., & Spinrad, T. L. (2016). Components of effortful control and their relations to children's shyness. *International Journal of Behavioral Development, 40*(6), 544–554. https://doi.org/10.1177/0165025415597792.

Eisenberg, N., Fabes, R. A., Shepard, S. A., Guthrie, I. K., Murphy, B. C., & Reiser, M. (1999). Parental reactions to children's negative emotions: Longitudinal relations to quality of children's social functioning. *Child Development, 70,* 513–534. https://doi.org/10.1111/1467-8624.00037.

Eisenberg, N., Cumberland, A., Spinrad, T. L., Fabes, R. A., Shepard, S. A., Reiser, M., . . . & Guthrie, I. K. (2001). The relations of regulation and emotionality to children's externalizing and internalizing problem behavior. *Child Development, 72*(4), 1112–1134. https://doi.org/10.1111/1467-8624.00337.

Eisenberg, N., Fabes, R. A., Guthrie, I. K., & Reiser, M. (2002). The role of emotionality and regulation in children' s social competence and adjustment. In L. Pulkkinen & A. Caspi (Eds.), *Paths to successful development: Personality in the life course* (pp. 46–70). New York: Cambridge University Press.

Eisenberg, N., Spinrad, T. L., Fabes, R. A., Reiser, M., Cumberland, A., Shepard, S. A., . . . & Thompson, M. (2004). The relations of effortful control and impulsivity to children's resiliency and adjustment. *Child Development, 75,* 25–46. https://doi.org/10.1111/j.1467-8624.2004.00652.x.

Eisenberg, N., Valiente, C., Spinrad, T. L., Cumberland, A., Liew, J., Reiser, M., . . . & Losoya, S. H. (2009). Longitudinal relations of children's effortful control, impulsivity, and negative emotionality to their externalizing, internalizing, and co-occurring behavior problems. *Developmental Psychology, 45*(4), 988–1008. https://doi.org/10.1037/a0016213.

Eisenberg, N., Duckworth, A. L., Spinrad, T. L., & Valiente, C. (2014). Conscientiousness: Origins in childhood? *Developmental Psychology, 50*(5), 1331–1349. https://doi.org/10.1037/a0030977.

Evans, G. W. (2003). A multimethodological analysis of cumulative risk and allostatic load among rural children. *Developmental Psychology, 39*(5), 924–933. https://doi.org/10.1037/0012-1649.39.5.924.

Evans, G. W., & Kim, P. (2012). Childhood poverty and young adults' allostatic load: The mediating role of childhood cumulative risk exposure. *Psychological Science, 23*(9), 979–983. https://doi.org/10.1177/0956797612441218.

Ezpeleta, L., Penelo, E., Osa, N., Navarro, J. B., & Trepat, E. (2019). Irritability and parenting practices as mediational variables between temperament and affective, anxiety, and oppositional defiant problems. *Aggressive Behavior, 45*(5), 550–560. https://doi.org/10.1002/ab.21850.

Farrell, A. H., & Vaillancourt, T. (2019). Temperament, bullying, and dating aggression: Longitudinal associations for adolescents in a romantic relationship. *Evolutionary Psychology, 17*(2). https://doi.org/10.1177/14747049 19847450.

Feldman, R., Keren, M., Gross-Rozval, O., & Tyano, S. (2004). Mother–child touch patterns in infant feeding disorders: Relation to maternal, child, and environmental factors. *Journal of the American Academy of Child & Adolescent Psychiatry, 43*, 1089–1097. https://doi.org/10.1097/01 .chi.0000132810.98922.83.

Ferguson, H. J., Brunsdon, V. E. A., & Bradford, E. E. F. (2021). The developmental trajectories of executive function from adolescence to old age. *Scientific Reports, 11*(1), 1382. https://doi.org/10.1038/s41598-020-80866-1.

Fosco, W. D., Hawk, L. W. Jr., Colder, C. R., Meisel, S. N., & Lengua, L. J. (2019). The development of inhibitory control in adolescence and prospective relations with delinquency. *Journal of Adolescence, 76*, 37–47. https://doi.org/10.1016/j.adolescence.2019.08.008.

Fox, N. A. (1994) Dynamic cerebral processes underlying emotion regulation. *Monographs of the Society for Research in Child Development, 59* (2/3), 152–166. https://doi.org/10.2307/1166143.

Fox, N. A., Henderson, H. A., Rubin, K. H., Calkins, S. D., & Schmidt, L. A. (2001). Continuity and discontinuity of behavioral inhibition and exuberance: Psychophysiological and behavioral influences across the first four years of life. *Child Development, 72*, 1–21. https://doi.org/10.1111/1467-8624.00262.

Froggatt, S., Covey, J., & Reissland, N. (2020). Infant neurobehavioural consequences of prenatal cigarette exposure: A systematic review and meta-analysis. *Acta Paediatrica, 109*(6), 1112–1124. https://doi.org/10.1111/apa.15132.

Frohn, S. R., Acar, I. H., Rudasill, K. M., Buhs, E. S., & Pérez-González, S. (2021). Temperament and social adjustment in first grade: The moderating role of teacher sensitivity. *Early Child Development and Care, 191*(9), 1427–1448. https://doi.org/10.1080/03004430.2019.1656618.

Fukkink, R. G. (2022). Infants in Dutch daycare: Exploring fine-grained dimensions of temperament. *Infant and Child Development, 31*(6), e2363. https://doi.org/10.1002/icd.2363.

Gable, P. A., Neal, L. B., & Threadgill, A. H. (2018). Regulatory behavior and frontal activity: Considering the role of revised-BIS in relative right frontal asymmetry. *Psychophysiology, 55*(1), e12910. https://doi.org/10.1111/psyp.12910.

Galler, J. R., Harrison, R. H., Ramsey, F., Butler, S., & Forde, V. (2004). Postpartum maternal mood, feeding practices, and infant temperament in Barbados. *Infant Behavior and Development, 27*, 267–287. https://doi.org/10.1016/j.infbeh.2003.11.002.

Garcia Coll, C., Kagan, J., & Reznick, J. S. (1984). Behavioral inhibition in young children. *Child Development, 55*, 1005–1019. https://doi.org/10.2307/1130152.

Gartstein, M. A. (2019). Frontal electroencephalogram (EEG) asymmetry: Exploring contributors to the still face procedure response. *International Journal of Behavioral Development, 44*, 193–204. https://doi.org/10.1177/0165025419850899.

Gartstein, M. A., & Skinner, M. K. (2018). Prenatal influences on temperament development: The role of environmental epigenetics. *Development and Psychopathology, 30*(4), 1269–1303. https://doi.org/10.1017/S0954579417001730.

Gartstein, M. A., Slobodskaya, H. R., Putnam, S. P., & Kinsht, I. A. (2009). A cross-cultural study of infant temperament: Predicting preschool effortful control in the United States of America (U.S.) and Russia. *European Journal of Developmental Psychology, 6*, 337–364. https://doi.org/10.1080/17405620701203846.

Gartstein, M. A., Bridgett, D. J., Rothbart, M. K., Robertson, C., Iddins, E., Ramsay, K., & Schlect, S. (2010). A latent growth examination of fear development in infancy: Contributions of maternal depression and the risk for toddler anxiety. *Developmental Psychology, 46*, 651–668. https://doi.org/10.1037/a0018898.

Gartstein, M. A., Putnam, S. P., & Rothbart, M. K. (2012). Etiology of preschool behavior problems: Contributions of temperament attributes in early childhood. *Infant Mental Health Journal, 33*(2), 197–211. https://doi.org/10.1002/imhj.21312.

Gartstein, M. A., Bridgett, D. J., Young, B. N., Panksepp, J., & Power, T. (2013). Origins of effortful control: Infant and parent contributions. *Infancy, 18*, 149–183. https://doi.org/10.1111/j.1532-7078.2012.00119.x.

Gartstein, M. A., Putnam, S. P., Aaron, E., & Rothbart, M. K. (2016). Temperament and personality. In S. Matzman (Ed.), *Oxford handbook of treatment processes and outcomes in counseling psychology* (pp. 11–41). New York: Oxford University Press.

Gartstein, M. A., Hancock, G. R., & Iverson, S. L. (2018). Positive affectivity and fear trajectories in infancy: Contributions of mother–child interaction factors. *Child Development*, *89*, 1519–1534. https://doi.org/10.1111/cdev.12843.

Gartstein, M. A., Hancock, G. R., Potapova, N. V., Calkins, S. D., & Bell, M. A. (2020). Modeling development of frontal electroencephalogram (EEG) asymmetry: Sex differences and links with temperament. *Developmental Science*, *23*, e12891. https://doi.org/10.1111/desc.12891.

Giedd J. N. (2012). The digital revolution and adolescent brain evolution. *Journal of Adolescent Health*, *51*(2), 101–105. https://doi.org/10.1016/j.jadohealth.2012.06.002.

Giedd, J. N. (2015). The amazing teen brain. *Scientific American*, *312*, 32–37. www.jstor.org/stable/26046640.

Gifford-Smith, M. E., & Brownell, C. A. (2003). Childhood peer relationships: Social acceptance, friendships, and peer networks. *Journal of School Psychology*, *41*(4), 235–284. https://doi.org/10.1016/S0022-4405(03)00048-7.

Glöggler, B., & Pauli-Pott, U. (2008). Different fear-regulation behaviors in toddlerhood: Relations to preceding infant negative emotionality, maternal depression, and sensitivity. *Merrill Palmer Quarterly*, *54*, 86–101. https://doi.org/10.1353/mpq.2008.0013.

Gölcük, M., & Berument, S. K. (2021). The relationship between negative parenting and child and maternal temperament. *Current Psychology*, *40*(7), 3596–3608. https://doi.org/10.1007/s12144-019-00307-9.

Goldsmith, H. H., & Campos, J. J. (1982). Toward a theory of infant temperament. In R. N. Emde & R. J. Harmon (Eds.),*The development of attachment and affiliative systems* (pp. 161–193). Boston, MA: Springer US.

Goldsmith, H. H., & Harman, C. (1994). Temperament and attachment: Individuals and relationships. *Current Directions in Psychological Science*, *3*(2), 53–57. https://doi.org/10.1111/1467-8721.ep10769948.

Goldsmith, H. H., Buss, A. H., Plomin, R., Rothbart, M. K., Thomas, A., Chess, S., ... & McCall, R. B. (1987). Roundtable: What is temperament? Four approaches. *Child Development*, *8*(2), 505–529. https://doi.org/10.2307/1130527.

Goldsmith, H. H., Lemery, K. S., Buss, K. A., & Campos, J. J. (1999). Genetic analyses of focal aspects of infant temperament. *Developmental Psychology*, *35*(4), 972–985. https://doi.org/10.1037/0012-1649.35.4.972.

Goodman, S. H., Rouse, M. H., Connell, A. M., Broth, M. R., Hall, C. M., & Heyward, D. (2011). Maternal depression and child psychopathology: A meta-analytic review. *Clinical Child and Family Psychology Review, 14*(1), 1–27. https://doi.org/10.1007/s10567-010-0080-1.

Goodrum, N. M., Smith, D. W., Hanson, R. F., Moreland, A. D., Saunders, B. E., & Kilpatrick, D. G. (2020). Longitudinal relations among adolescent risk behavior, family cohesion, violence exposure, and mental health in a national sample. *Journal of Abnormal Child Psychology, 48*(11), 1455–1469. https://doi.org/10.1007/s10802-020-00691-y.

Gouge, N., Dixon, W. E. Jr., Driggers-Jones, L. P., & Price, J. S. (2020). Cumulative sociodemographic risk indicators for difficult child temperament. *Journal of Genetic Psychology, 181*(1), 32–37. https://doi.org/10.1080/0022 1325.2019.1699012.

Graber, J. A., Nichols, T. R., Brooks-Gunn, J. (2010). Putting pubertal timing in developmental context: Implications for prevention. *Developmental Psychobiology, 52*, 254–262. https://doi.org/10.1002/dev.20438.

Gray, J. A., & McNaughton, N. (1996). The neuropsychology of anxiety: Reprise. In D. A. Hope (Ed.), *Nebraska Symposium on Motivation, 1995: Perspectives on anxiety, panic, and fear* (pp. 61–134). Lincoln, NE: University of Nebraska Press.

Gray, J. A., & McNaughton, N. (2000). *The neuropsychology of anxiety.* Oxford: Oxford University Press.

Graziano, P., & Derefinko, K. (2013). Cardiac vagal control and children's adaptive functioning: A meta-analysis. *Biological Psychology, 94*(1), 22–37. https://doi.org/10.1016/j.biopsycho.2013.04.011.

Groh, A. M., Narayan, A. J., Bakermans-Kranenburg, M. J., Roisman, G. I., Vaughn, B. E., Fearon, R. P., & van IJzendoorn, M. H. (2017). Attachment and temperament in the early life course: A meta-analytic review. *Child Development, 88*(3), 770–795. https://doi.org/10.1111/cdev.12677.

Gudiño, O. G., & Lau, A. S. (2010). Parental cultural orientation, shyness, and anxiety in Hispanic children: An exploratory study. *Journal of Applied Developmental Psychology, 31*, 202–210. https://doi.org/10.1016/j.appdev.2009 .12.003.

Gunnar, M. R., Sebanc, A. M., Tout, K., Donzella, B., & van Dulmen, M. M. H. (2003). Peer rejection, temperament, and cortisol activity in preschoolers. *Developmental Psychobiology, 43*, 346–358. https://doi.org/10.1002/dev.10144.

Gys, C. L., Haft, S. L., & Zhou, Q. (2024). Relations between self-regulation and behavioral adjustment in Chinese American immigrant children during early elementary school years. *Child Development, 95*(1), 160–176. https://doi.org/10.1111/cdev.13981.

Haddad, J. D., Barocas, R., & Hollenbeck, A. R. (1991). Family organization and parent attitudes of children with conduct disorder. *Journal of Clinical Child Psychology*, *20*(2), 152–161. https://doi.org/10.1207/s15374424j ccp2002_6.

Haley, D. W., Handmaker, N. S., & Lowe, J. (2006). Infant stress reactivity and prenatal alcohol exposure. *Alcoholism: Clinical and Experimental Research*, *30*, 2055–2064. https://doi.org/10.1111/j.1530-0277.2006.00251.x.

Halvorson, M. A., King, K. M. & Lengua, L. J. (2022). Examining interactions between negative emotionality and effortful control in predicting preadolescent adjustment. *Journal of Applied Developmental Psychology*, *79*, 101374. https://doi.org/10.1016/j.appdev.2021.101374.

Hane, A. A., Fox, N. A., Henderson, H. A., & Marshall, P. J. (2008). Behavioral reactivity and approach-withdrawal bias in infancy. *Developmental Psychology*, *44*, 1491–1496. https://doi.org/10.1037/a0012855.

Hanington, L., Ramchandani, P., & Stein, A. (2010). Parental depression and child temperament: Assessing child to parent effects in a longitudinal population study. *Infant Behavior and Development*, *33*(1), 88–95. https://doi.org/10.1016/j.infbeh.2009.11.004.

Hardin, J. S., Jones, N. A., Mize, K. D., & Platt, M. (2021). Affectionate touch in the context of breastfeeding and maternal depression influences infant neurodevelopmental and temperamental substrates. *Neuropsychobiology*, *80*(2), 158–175. https://doi.org/10.1159/000511604.

Hardway, C., Kagan, J., Snidman, N., & Pincus, D. B. (2013). Infant reactivity as a predictor of child anxiety, social ease, and parenting behavior in middle childhood. *Journal of Psychopathology and Behavior Assessment*, *35*, 531–539. https://doi.org/10.1007/s10862-013-9362-5.

Harkness, S., & Super, C. M. (1994). The "developmental niche": A theoretical framework for analyzing the household production of health. *Social Science and Medicine*, *38*(2), 217–226. https://doi.org/10.1016/0277-9536(94) 90391-3.

Hart, D., Atkins, R., & Matsuba, M. K. (2008). The association of neighborhood poverty with personality change in childhood. *Journal of Personality and Social Psychology*, *94*(6), 1048–1061. https://doi.org/10.1037/0022-3514.94.6.1048.

Heim C., & Nemeroff, C. B. (1999). The impact of early adverse experiences on brain systems involved in the pathophysiology of anxiety and affective disorders. *Biological Psychiatry*, *46*(11), 1509–1522. https://doi.org/10.1016/S0066-3223(99)00224-3.

Heim C., Ehlert U., & Hellhammer D. K. (2000). The potential role of hypocortisolism in the pathophysiology of stress-related bodily disorders.

Psychoneuroendocrinology, *25*, 1–35. https://doi.org/10.1016/S0306-4530 (99)00035-9.

Heiman, N., Stallings, M. C., Hofer, S. M., & Hewitt, J. K. (2003). Investigating age differences in the genetic and environmental structure of the tridimensional personality questionnaire in later adulthood. *Behavior Genetics*, *33*, 171–180. https://doi.org/10.1023/A:1022558002760.

Heiman, N., Stallings, M. C., Young, S. E., & Hewitt, J. K. (2004). Investigating the genetic and environmental structure of Cloninger's personality dimensions in adolescence. *Twin Research and Human Genetics*, *7*, 462–470. https://doi.org/10.1375/twin.7.5.462.

Hentges, R. F., Davies, P. T., & Cicchetti, D. (2015). Temperament and interparental conflict: The role of negative emotionality in predicting child behavioral problems. *Child Development*, *86*(5), 1333–1350. https://doi.org/ 10.1111/cdev.12389.

Hernández-Martíenz, C., Canals, J., Aranda, N., Ribot, B., Escribano, J., & Arija, V. (2011). Effects of iron deficiency on neonatal behavior at different stages of pregnancy. *Early Human Development*, *87*, 165–169. https://doi .org/10.1016/j.earlhumdev.2010.12.006.

Hittner, J. B., Tripicchio, C. & Faith, G. (2016). Infant emotional distress, maternal restriction at a home meal, and child BMI gain through age 6 years in the Colorado Adoption Project. *Eating Behaviors*, *21*, 135–141. https://doi.org/10.1016/j.eatbeh.2016.01.008.

Hoffmann, M. S., Pan, P. M., Manfro, G. G., de Jesus Mari, J., Miguel, E. C., Bressan, R.A., . . . & Salum, G. A. (2019). Cross-sectional and longitudinal associations of temperament and mental disorders in youth. *Child Psychiatry and Human Development*, *50*(3), 374–383. https://doi.org/10.1007/s10578-018-0846-0.

Hofstede, G., Hofstede, G. J., & Minkov, M. (2010). *Cultures and organizations: Software of the mind*, rev. ed. New York: McGraw-Hill.

Hofstee, M., Huijding, J., Cuevas, K., & Deković, M. (2022). Self-regulation and frontal EEG alpha activity during infancy and early childhood: A multilevel meta-analysis. *Developmental Science*, *25*(6), e13298. https:// doi.org/10.1111/desc.13298.

Huffman, L. C., Bryan, Y. E., del Carmen, R., Pederson, F. A., Doussard-Roosevelt, J. A., & Porges, S. W. (1998). Infant temperament and cardiac vagal tone: Assessments at twelve weeks of age. *Child Development*, *69*, 624–635. https://doi.org/10.1111/j.1467-8624.1998.tb06233.x.

Iverson, S. L., & Gartstein, M. A. (2018). Applications of temperament: A review of caregiver-focused temperament-driven interventions. *Early*

Education and Development, 29(1), 31–52. https://doi.org/10.1080/10409289.2017.1341805.

James, A. G., Coard, S. I., Fine, M. A., & Rudy, D. (2018). The central roles of race and racism in reframing family systems theory: A consideration of choice and time. *Journal of Family Theory & Review, 10*(2), 419–433. https://doi.org/10.1111/jftr.12262.

Jones, S. C., Anderson, R. E., & Stevenson, H. C. (2021). Not the same old song and dance: Viewing racial socialization through a family systems lens to resist racial trauma. *Adversity and Resilience Science, 2*, 225–233. https://doi.org/10.1007/s42844-021-00044-8.

Kagan, J. (1998). Biology and the child. In W. Damon & N. Eisenberg (Eds.), *Handbook of child psychology: Social, emotional, and personality development*, 5th ed. (pp. 177–235). Hoboken, NJ: John Wiley & Sons.

Kagan, J., & Fox, N. A. (2006). Biology, culture, and temperamental biases. In N. Eisenberg, W. Damon, & R. Lerner (Eds.), *Handbook of child psychology: Vol. 3, Social, emotional, and personality development*, 6th ed. (pp. 167–225). Hoboken, NJ: John Wiley & Sons.

Kagan, J., & Snidman, N. (2004). *The long shadow of temperament.* Cambridge, MA.: Harvard University Press.

Kälin, S., & Roebers, C. M. (2021). Self-regulation in preschool children: Factor structure of different measures of effortful control and executive functions. *Journal of Cognition and Development, 22*(1), 48–67. https://doi.org/10.1080/15248372.2020.1862120.

Kapetanovic, S., Zietz, S., Lansford, J. E., Bacchini, D., Bornstein, M. H., Chang, L., ... & Al-Hassan, S. M. (2023). Parenting, adolescent sensation seeking, and subsequent substance use: Moderation by adolescent temperament. *Journal of Youth and Adolescence, 52*(6), 1235–1254. https://doi.org/10.1007/s10964-023-01765-y.

Keating, D. P. (2012). Cognitive and brain development in adolescence. *Enfance, 64*(3), 267–279.

Keijsers, L., & Poulin, F. (2013). Developmental changes in parent–child communication throughout adolescence. *Developmental Psychology, 49*(12), 2301. https://doi.org/10.1037/a0032217.

Kelmanson, I. (2004). Temperament and sleep characteristics in two-month-old infants. *Sleep and Hypnosis: A Journal of Clinical Neuroscience and Psychopathology, 6*(2), 67–73. www.sleepandhypnosis.org/ing/abstract.aspx?MkID=134.

Kerr, M. E., & Bowen, M. (1988). *Family evaluation.* New York: W. W. Norton & Company.

Kids Count Data Center (2022). Children in poverty by race and ethnicity in the united states. Annie E. Casey Foundation. https://bit.ly/44m72oL.

Kiel, E. J., & Buss, K. A. (2012). Associations among context-specific maternal protective behavior, toddler fearful temperament, and maternal accuracy and goals. *Social Development, 21*, 742–760. https://doi.org/10.1111/j.1467-9507.2011.00645.x.

Kiff, C. J., Lengua, L. J., & Zalewski, M. (2011). Nature and nurturing: Parenting in the context of child temperament. *Clinical Child and Family Psychology Review, 14*, 251–301. https://doi.org/10.1007/s10567-011-0093-4.

Kim, J., Rapee, M. R., Oh, J. K., & Moon, H. S. (2008). Retrospective report of social withdrawal during adolescence and current maladjustment in young adulthood: Cross-cultural comparisons between Australian and South Korean students. *Journal of Adolescence, 31*, 543–563. https://doi.org/10.1016/j.adolescence.2007.10.011.

Kim, S., & Kochanska, G. (2020). Family sociodemographic resources moderate the path from toddlers' hard-to-manage temperament to parental control to disruptive behavior in middle childhood. *Development and Psychopathology, 33*(1), 160–172. https://doi.org/10.1017/S0954579419001664.

Kim-Spoon, J., Deater-Deckard, K., Holmes, C., Lee, J., Chiu, P., & King-Casas, B. (2016). Behavioral and neural inhibitory control moderates the effects of reward sensitivity on adolescent substance use. *Neuropsychologia, 91*, 318–326. https://doi.org/10.1016/j.neuropsychologia.2016.08.028.

Kim-Spoon, J., Deater-Deckard, K., Calkins, S. D., King-Casas, B., & Bell, M. A. (2019). Commonality between executive functioning and effortful control related to adjustment. *Journal of Applied Developmental Psychology, 60*, 47–55. https://doi.org/10.1016/j.appdev.2018.10.004.

Kirschbaum, C., Ehlert, U., Piedmont, E., & Hellhammer, D. H. (1990). Postpartum blues: Salivary cortisol and psychological factors. *Journal of Psychosomatic Research, 34*, 319–325. https://doi.org/10.1016/0022-3999(90)90088-L.

Kishiyama, M. M., Boyce, W. T., Jimenez, A. M., Perry, L. M., & Knight, R. T. (2009). Socioeconomic disparities affect prefrontal function in children. *Journal of Cognitive Neuroscience, 21*(6), 1106–1115. https://doi.org/10.1162/jocn.2009.21101.

Klein, M. R., Lengua, L. J., Thompson, S. F., Moran, L., Ruberry, E. J., Kiff, C., & Zalewski, M. (2018). Bidirectional relations between temperament and parenting predicting preschool-age children's adjustment. *Journal of Clinical Child & Adolescent Psychology, 47*, S113–S126. https://doi.org/10.1080/15374416.2016.1169537.

Knyazev, G. G., Savostyanov, A. N., Bocharov, A. V., Slobodskaya, H. R., Bairova, N. B., Tamozhnikov, S. S., & Stepanova, V. V. (2017). Effortful control and resting state networks: A longitudinal EEG study. *Neuroscience, 346*, 365–381. https://doi.org/10.1016/j.neuroscience.2017.01.031.

Kochanska, G. (1995). Children's temperament, mothers' discipline, and security of attachment: Multiple pathways to emerging internalization. *Child Development, 66*, 597–615. https://doi.org/10.1111/j.1467-8624.1995.tb00892.x.

Kochanska, G. (1997). Multiple pathways to conscience for children with different temperaments: From toddlerhood to age 5. *Developmental Psychology, 33*, 228–240. https://doi.org/10.1037/0012-1649.33.2.228.

Kochanska, G., & Knaak, A. (2003). Effortful control as a personality characteristic of young children: Antecedents, correlates, and consequences. *Journal of Personality, 71*, 1087–1112. https://doi.org/10.1111/1467-6494.7106008.

Kochanska, G., Coy, K., & Murray, K. (2001). The development of self-regulation in the first four years of life. *Child Development, 72*, 1091–1111. https://doi.org/10.1111/1467-8624.00336.

Kochanska, G., Aksan, N., & Joy, M. (2007). Children's fearfulness as a moderator of parenting in early socialization: Two longitudinal studies. *Developmental Psychology, 43*, 222–237. https://doi.org/10.1037/0012-1649.43.1.222.

Kolb, B. (2018). Brain plasticity and experience. In R. Gibb & B. Kolb (Eds.), *The neurobiology of brain and behavioral development* (pp. 341–389). Ebook. Elsevier Academic Press. https://doi.org/10.1016/B978-0-12-804036-2.00013-3.

Kopala-Sibley, D. C., Olino, T., Durbin, E., Dyson, M. W., & Klein, D. N. (2018). The stability of temperament from early childhood to early adolescence: A multi-method, multi-informant examination. *European Journal of Personality, 32*(2), 128–145. https://doi.org/10.1002/per.2151.

Koss, K. J., Mliner, S. B., Donzella, B., & Gunnar, M. R. (2016). Early adversity, hypocortisolism, and behavior problems at school entry: A study of internationally adopted children. *Psychoneuroendocrinology, 66*, 31–38. https://doi.org/10.1016/j.psyneuen.2015.12.018.

Krassner, A., Gartstein, M. A., Park, C., Dragan, W. L., Lecannelier, F., & Putnam, S. P. (2017). East–west, collectivist–individualist: A cross-cultural examination of temperament in toddlers from Chile, Poland, South Korea, and the U.S. *European Journal of Developmental Psychology, 14*, 449–464. https://doi.org/10.1080/17405629.2016.1236722.

Laceulle, O. M., Nederhof, E., Karreman, A., Ormel, J., & van Aken, M. A. G. (2012). Stressful events and temperament change during early and middle adolescence: The TRAILS study. *European Journal of Personality, 26*(3), 276–284. https://doi.org/10.1002/per.832.

Lacey, M. F., Neal, L. B., & Gable, P. A. (2020). Effortful control of motivation, not withdrawal motivation, relates to greater right frontal asymmetry. *International Journal of Psychophysiology, 147,* 18–25. https://doi.org/10.1016/j.ijpsycho.2019.09.013.

Landry, S. H., & Smith, K. E. (2010). Early social and cognitive precursors and parental support for self-regulation and executive function: Relations from early childhood into adolescence. In B. W. Sokol, U. Müller, J. I. M. Carpendale, A. R. Young, & G. Iarocci (Eds.), *Self- and social-regulation: Exploring the relations between social interaction, social understanding, and the development of executive functions* (pp. 385–417). New York: Oxford Academic. https://doi.org/10.1093/acprof:oso/9780195327694.003.0016.

Lawson, K. M., Kellerman, J. K., Kleiman, E. M., Bleidorn, W., Hopwood, C. J., & Robins, R. W. (2022). The role of temperament in the onset of suicidal ideation and behaviors across adolescence: Findings from a 10-year longitudinal study of Mexican-origin youth. *Journal of Personality and Social Psychology, 122*(1), 171–186. https://doi.org/10.1037/pspp0000382.

Leerkes, E. M., Blankson, A. N., & O'Brien, M. (2009). Differential effects of maternal sensitivity to infant distress and nondistress on social-emotional functioning. *Child Development, 80*(3), 762–775. https://doi.org/10.1111/j.1467-8624.2009.01296.x.

Leerkes, E. M., Weaver, J. M., & O'Brien, M. (2012). Differentiating maternal sensitivity to infant distress and non-distress. *Parenting, 12*(2–3), 175–184. https://doi.org/10.1080/15295192.2012.683353.

Lemery-Chalfant, K., Doelger, L., & Goldsmith, H. H. (2008). Genetic relations between effortful and attentional control and symptoms of psychopathology in middle childhood. *Infant and Child Development: An International Journal of Research and Practice, 17*(4), 365–385. https://doi.org/10.1002/icd.581.

Lengua, L. J. (2006). Growth in temperament and parenting as predictors of adjustment during children's transition to adolescence. *Developmental Psychology, 42*(5), 819–832. https://doi.org/10.1037/0012-1649.42.5.819.

Lengua, L. J., & Kovacs, E. A. (2005). Bidirectional associations between temperament and parenting, and the prediction of adjustment problems in middle childhood. *Journal of Applied Developmental Psychology, 26,* 21–38. https://doi.org/10.1016/j.appdev.2004.10.001.

Lengua, L. J., & Wachs, T. D. (2012). Temperament and risk: Resilient and vulnerable responses to adversity. In M. Zentner & R. Shiner (Eds.), *The handbook of temperament* (pp. 519–540). New York: Guilford Press.

Lengua, L. J., Sandler, I. N., West, S. G., Wolchik, S. A., & Curran, P. J. (1999). Emotionality and self-regulation, threat appraisal, and coping in children of divorce. *Development and Psychopathology, 11*(1), 15–37. https://doi.org/ 10.1017/S0954579499001935.

Lengua, L. J., Kiff, C., Moran, L., Zalewski, M., Thompson, S., Cortes, R., & Ruberry, E. (2014). Parenting mediates the effects of income and cumulative risk on the development of effortful control. *Social Development, 23*(3), 631–649. https://doi.org/10.1111/sode.12071.

Lengua, L. J., Moran, L., Zalewski, M., Ruberry, E., Kiff, C., & Thompson, S. (2015). Relations of growth in effortful control to family income, cumulative risk, and adjustment in preschool-age children. *Journal of Abnormal Child Psychology, 43*, 705–720. https://doi.org/10.1007/s10802-014-9941-2.

Lengua, L. J., Thompson, S. F., Moran, L. R., Zalewski, M., Ruberry, E. J., Klein, M. R., & Kiff, C. J. (2020). Pathways from early adversity to later adjustment: Tests of the additive and bidirectional effects of executive control and diurnal cortisol in early childhood. *Development and Psychopathology, 32*(2), 545–558. https://doi.org/10.1017/S0954579419000373.

Lensing, N., & Elsner, B. (2018). Development of hot and cool executive functions in middle childhood: Three-year growth curves of decision making and working memory updating. *Journal of Experimental Child Psychology, 173*, 187–204. https://doi.org/10.1016/j.jecp.2018.04.002.

Lerner, R. M., Johnson, S. K., & Buckingham, M. H. (2015). Relational developmental systems-based theories and the study of children and families: Lerner and Spanier (1978) revisited. *Journal of Family Theory & Review, 7* (2), 83–104. https://doi.org/10.1111/jftr.12067.

Leve, L. D., Griffin, A. M., Natsuaki, M. N., Harold, G. T., Neiderhiser, J. M., Ganiban, J. M., ... & Reiss, D. (2019). Longitudinal examination of pathways to peer problems in middle childhood: A siblings-reared-apart design. *Development and Psychopathology, 31*(5), 1633–1647. https://doi.org/ 10.1017/S0954579419000890.

Lewinsohn, P. M., Steinmetz, J. L., Larson, D. W., & Franklin, J. (1981). Depression-related cognitions: Antecedent or consequence? *Journal of Abnormal Psychology, 90*(3), 213–219. https://doi.org/10.1017/S09545 79419000890.

Li, W., & Zinbarg, R. E. (2007). Anxiety sensitivity and panic attacks: A 1-year longitudinal study. *Behavior Modification, 31*(2), 145–161. https://doi.org/ 10.1177/0145445506296969.

Licht, C., Mortensen, E. L., & Knudsen, G. M. (2011). Association between sensory processing sensitivity and the serotonin transporter polymorphism 5-HTTLPR short/short genotype. *Biological Psychiatry, 69*, 152S–153S.

Lin, B., Liew, J., & Perez, M. (2019). Measurement of self-regulation in early childhood: Relations between laboratory and performance-based measures of effortful control and executive functioning. *Early Childhood Research Quarterly, 47,* 1–8. https://doi.org/10.1016/j.ecresq.2018.10.004.

Lin, B., Lemery-Chalfant, K., Beekman, C., Crnic, K. A., Gonzales, N. A., & Luecken, L. J. (2021). Infant temperament profiles, cultural orientation, and toddler behavioral and physiological regulation in Mexican-American families. *Child Development, 92*(6), e1110–e1125. https://doi.org/10.1111/cdev.13637.

Linehan, M. M. (2014). *DBT training manual.* New York: Guilford Press.

Linver, M. R., Brooks-Gunn, J., & Kohen, D. E. (2002).Family processes as pathways from income to young children's development. *Developmental Psychology, 38*(5), 719–734. https://doi.org/10.1037/0012-1649.38.5.719.

Liu, P., Kryski, K., Smith, H., Joanisse, M., & Hayden, E. (2019). Transactional relations between early child temperament, structured parenting, and child outcomes: A three-wave longitudinal study. *Development and Psychopathology, 32,* 923–933. https://doi.org/10.1017/S0954579419000841.

Loman, M. M., & Gunnar, M. R. (2010). Early experience and the development of stress reactivity and regulation in children. *Neuroscience and Biobehavioral Reviews, 34,* 867–876. https://doi.org/10.1016/j.neubiorev.2009.05.007.

Lucia V. C., & Breslau N. (2006). Family cohesion and children's behavior problems: A longitudinal investigation. *Psychiatry Research, 141*(2), 141–149. https://doi.org/10.1016/j.psychres.2005.06.009.

Luciana, M., & Collins, P. F. (2012). Incentive motivation, cognitive control, and the adolescent brain: Is it time for a paradigm shift? *Child Development Perspectives, 6*(4), 392–399. https://doi.org/10.1111/j.1750-8606.2012.00252.x.

Manlove, E. E., & Vernon-Feagans, L. (2002). Caring for infant daughters and sons in dual-earner households: Maternal reports of father involvement in weekday time and tasks. *Infant and Child Development, 11,* 305–320. https://doi.org/10.1002/icd.260.

Marceau, K., Rolan, E., Leve, L. D., Ganiban, J. M., Reiss, D., Shaw, D. S., . . . & Neiderhiser, J. M. (2019). Parenting and prenatal risk as moderators of genetic influences on conduct problems during middle childhood. *Developmental Psychology, 55*(6), 1164–1181. https://doi.org/10.1037/dev0000701.

Marcovitch, S., Clearfield, M. W., Swingler, M., Calkins, S. D., & Bell, M. A. (2016). Attentional predictors of 5-month-olds' performance on a looking A-not-B task. *Infant and Child Development, 25*(4), 233–246. https://doi.org/10.1002/icd.1931.

Mauer, E., Zhou, Q., & Uchikoshi, Y. (2021). A longitudinal study on bidirectional relations between executive functions and English word-level reading in Chinese American children in immigrant families. *Learning and Individual Differences*, *86*, 101976. https://doi.org/10.1016/j.lindif.2021.101976.

McBride, B. A., & Mills, G. (1993). A comparison of mother and father involvement with their preschool children. *Early Childhood Research Quarterly*, *8*, 457–477. https://doi.org/10.1016/S0885-2006(05)80080-8.

McClowry, S. G., & Collins, A. (2012). Temperament-based intervention: Reconceptualized from a response-to-intervention framework. In M. Zentner & R. L. Shiner (Eds.), *Handbook of temperament* (pp. 581–603). New York: Guilford Press.

McCormick, M. P., Turbeville, A. R., Barnes, S. P., & McClowry, S. G. (2014). Challenging temperament, teacher–child relationships, and behavior problems in urban low-income children: A longitudinal examination. *Early Education and Development*, *25*(8), 1198–1218. https://doi.org/10.1080/10409289.2014.915676.

McCrae, R. R., & John, O. P. (1992). An introduction to the five-factor model and its applications. *Journal of Personality*, *60*(2), 175–215. https://doi.org/10.1111/j.1467-6494.1992.tb00970.x.

McLoyd, V. C. (1990). The impact of economic hardship on Black families and children: Psychological distress, parenting, and socioemotional development. *Child Development*, *61*(2), 311–346. https://doi.org/10.1111/j.1467-8624.1990.tb02781.x.

Mehall, K. G., Spinrad, T. L., Eisenberg, N., & Gaertner, B. M. (2009). Examining the relations of infant temperament and couples' marital satisfaction to mother and father involvement: A longitudinal study. *Fathering*, *7*(1), 23–48. https://doi.org/10.3149/fth.0701.23.

Mistry, R. S., Vandewater, E. A., Huston, A. C., & McLoyd, V. C. (2002). Economic well-being and children's social adjustment: The role of family process in an ethnically diverse low-income sample. *Child Development*, *73*(3), 935–951. https://doi.org/10.1111/1467-8624.00448.

Moore, M., Slane, J., Mindell, J. A., Burt, S. A., & Klump, K. L. (2011). Sleep problems and temperament in adolescents. *Child: Care, Health and Development*, *37*(4), 559–562. https://doi.org/10.1111/j.1365-2214.2010.01157.x

Morales-Munoz, I., Nolvi, S., Virta, M., Karlsson, H., Paavonen, E. J., & Karlsson, L. (2020). The longitudinal associations between temperament and sleep during the first year of life. *Infant Behavior and Development*, *61*, 101485. https://doi.org/10.1016/j.infbeh.2020.101485.

Moran, L., Lengua, L. J., Zalewski, M., Ruberry, E., Klein, M., Thompson, S., & Kiff, C. (2017). Variable-and person-centered approaches to examining temperament vulnerability and resilience to the effects of contextual risk. *Journal of Research in Personality, 67,* 61–74. https://doi.org/10.1016/j.jrp.2016.03.003.

Morrell, J., & Steele, H. (2003). The role of attachment security, temperament, maternal perception, and care-giving behavior in persistent infant sleeping problems. *Infant Mental Health Journal, 24,* 447–468. https://doi.org/10.1002/imhj.10072.

Mrug, S., Molina, B. S., Hoza, B., Gerdes, A. C., Hinshaw, S. P., Hechtman, L., & Arnold, L. E. (2012). Peer rejection and friendships in children with attention-deficit/hyperactivity disorder: Contributions to long-term outcomes. *Journal of Abnormal Child Psychology, 40,* 1013–1026. https://doi.org/10.1007/s10802-012-9610-2.

Murphy, B. C., Shepard, S. A., Eisenberg, N., Fabes, R. A., & Guthrie, I. K. (1999). Contemporaneous and longitudinal relations of dispositional sympathy to emotionality, regulation, and social functioning. *Journal of Early Adolescence, 19*(1), 66–97. https://doi.org/10.1177/0272431699019001004.

Murphy, B. C., Shepard, S. A., Eisenberg, N., & Fabes, R. A. (2004). Concurrent and across time prediction of young adolescents' social functioning: The role of emotionality and regulation. *Social Development, 13*(1), 56–86. https://doi.org/10.1111/j.1467-9507.2004.00257.x.

Myerberg, L. B., Rabinowitz, J. A., Reynolds, M. D., & Drabick, D. A. G. (2019). Does negative emotional reactivity moderate the relation between contextual cohesion and adolescent well-being? *Journal of Youth and Adolescence, 48* (11), 2179–2189. https://doi.org/10.1007/s10964-019-01053-8.

National Longitudinal Surveys. (n.d.) National Longitudinal Survey of Youth, NLYS97. Bureau of Labor Statistics, U.S. Department of Labor. www.nlsinfo.org/content/cohorts/nlsy97.

Nelson, B. W., Byrne, M. L., Simmons, J. G., Whittle, S., Schwartz, O. S., O'Brien-Simpson, N. M., ... & Allen, N. B. (2018). Adolescent temperament dimensions as stable prospective risk and protective factors for salivary C-reactive protein. *British Journal of Health Psychology, 23*(1), 186–207. https://doi.org/10.1111/bjhp.12281.

Neumann, A., Barker, E. D., Koot, H. M., & Maughan, B. (2010). The role of contextual risk, impulsivity, and parental knowledge in the development of adolescent antisocial behavior. *Journal of Abnormal Psychology, 119*(3), 534–545. https://doi.org/10.1037/a0019860.

Niegel, S., Ystrom, E., & Vollrath, M. E. (2007). Is difficult temperament related to overweight and rapid early weight gain in infants? A prospective cohort study. *Journal of Developmental and Behavioral Pediatrics, 28,* 462–466. https://doi.org/10.1097/DBP.0b013e31811431e8.

Nigg, J. T. (2006). Temperament and developmental psychopathology. *Journal of Child Psychology and Psychiatry, 47*(3–4), 395–422. https://doi.org/10.1111/j.1469-7610.2006.01612.x.

Nigg, J. T. (2017). Annual research review: On the relations among self-regulation, self-control, executive functioning, effortful control, cognitive control, impulsivity, risk-taking, and inhibition for developmental psychopathology. *Journal of Child Psychology and Psychiatry, 58*(4), 361–383. https://doi.org/10.1111/jcpp.12675.

Nolvi, S., Karlsson, L., Bridgett, D. J., Korja, R., Huizink, A. C., Kataja, E. L., & Karlsson, H. (2016). Maternal prenatal stress and infant emotional reactivity six months postpartum. *Journal of Affective Disorders, 199*, 163–170. https://doi.org/10.1016/j.jad.2016.04.020.

Padilla, C. M., & Ryan, R. M. (2019). The link between child temperament and low-income mothers' and fathers' parenting. *Infant Mental Health Journal, 40*(2), 217–233. https://doi.org/10.1002/imhj.21770.

Pagliaccio, D., Luking, K. R., Anokhin, A. P., Gotlib, I. H., Hayden, E. P., Olino, T. M., . . . & Barch, D. M. (2016). Revising the BIS/BAS Scale to study development: Measurement invariance and normative effects of age and sex from childhood through adulthood. *Psychological Assessment, 28*(4), 429–442. https://doi.org/10.1037/pas0000186.

Panter-Brick, C. (2015). Culture and resilience: Next steps for theory and practice. In L. C. Theron, L. Liebenberg, & M. Ungar (Eds.), *Youth resilience and culture: Commonalities and complexities* (pp. 233–244). Dordrecht: Springer Science + Business Media. https://doi.org/10.1007/978-94-017-9415-2_17.

Parade, S. H., & Leerkes, E. M. (2008). The reliability and validity of the Infant Behavior Questionnaire-Revised. *Infant Behavior and Development, 31*, 637–646. https://doi.org/10.1016/j.infbeh.2008.07.009.

Parade, S. H., Armstrong, L. M., Dickstein, S., & Seifer, R. (2018). Family context moderates the association of maternal postpartum depression and stability of infant temperament. *Child Development, 89*(6), 2118–2135. https://doi.org/10.1111/cdev.12895.

Park, S. Y., Belsky, J., Putnam, S., & Crnic, K. (1997). Infant emotionality, parenting, and 3-year inhibition: Exploring stability and lawful discontinuity in a male sample. *Developmental Psychology, 33*(2), 218–227. https://doi.org/10.1037/0012-1649.33.2.218.

Parrish, K. H., Thompson, S. F., & Lengua, L. J. (2021) Temperament as a moderator of the association of cumulative risk with preadolescent appraisal and coping style. *Anxiety, Stress, & Coping, 34*(5), 513–529. https://doi.org/10.1080/10615806.2021.1918681.

Pistella, J., Zava, F., Sette, S., Baumgartner, E., & Baiocco, R. (2020). Peer victimization, social functioning, and temperament traits in preschool children: The role of gender, immigrant status and sympathy. *Child Indicators Research, 13*(6), 2135–2156. https://doi.org/10.1007/s12187-020-09736-6.

Pluess, M. (2017). Vantage sensitivity: Environmental sensitivity to positive experiences as a function of genetic differences. *Journal of Personality, 85* (1), 38–50. https://doi.org/10.1111/jopy.12218.

Pluess, M., & Belsky, J. (2009). Differential susceptibility to rearing experience: The case of childcare. *Journal of Child Psychology and Psychiatry, 50* (4), 396–404. https://doi.org/10.1111/j.1469–7610.2008.01992.x.

Polo, A. J., & Lopez, S. R. (2009). Culture, context and the internalizing distress of Mexican American youth. *Journal of Clinical Child and Adolescent Psychology, 38*, 273–285. https://doi.org/10.1080/15374410802698370.

Poon, K. (2018). Hot and cool executive functions in adolescence: Development and contributions to important developmental outcomes. *Frontiers in Psychology, 8*, 306175. https://doi.org/10.3389/fpsyg.2017 .02311.

Popp, T. K., Spinrad, T. L., & Smith, C. L. (2008). The relation of cumulative demographic risk to mothers' responsivity and control: Examining the role of toddler temperament. *Infancy, 13*(5), 496–518. https://doi.org/10.1080/ 15250000802329446.

Porges, S. W. (1997). Emotion: an evolutionary by-product of the neural regulation of the autonomic nervous system. *Annals of the New York Academy of Sciences, 807*, 62–77.

Porges, S. W. (2011). *The polyvagal theory: Neurophysiological foundations of emotions, attachment, communication, and self-regulation*. New York: Norton.

Posner, M. I., Rothbart, M. K., Sheese, B. E., & Voelker P. (2012). Control networks and neuromodulators of early development. *Developmental Psychology, 48*, 827–835. https://doi.org/10.1037/a0025530.

Putnam, S. P., & Gartstein, M. A. (2017). Aggregate temperament scores from multiple countries: Associations with aggregate personality traits, cultural dimensions, and allelic frequency. *Journal of Research in Personality, 67*, 157–170. https://doi.org/10.1016/j.jrp.2016.07.009.

Putnam, S. P., Rothbart, M. K., & Gartstein, M. A. (2008). Homotypic and heterotypic continuity of fine-grained temperament during infancy, toddlerhood, and early childhood. *Infant and Child Development, 17*, 387–405. https://doi.org/10.1002/icd.582.

Putnam, S. P., Selec, E., French, B., Gartstein, M. A., Lira Luttges, B., & 489 members of the Global Temperament Project (2024). The Global

Temperament Project: Parent-reported temperament in infants, toddlers and children from 59 nations. *Developmental Psychology*. Advance online publication. https://doi.org/10.1037/dev0001732.

Qian, G., Chen, X., Jiang, S., Guo, X., Tian, L., & Dou, G. (2022). Temperament and sibling relationships: The mediating effect of social competence and behavior. *Current Psychology*, *41*(9), 6147–6153. https://doi.org/10.1007/s12144-020-01080-w.

Quinn, P. D., & Harden, K. P. (2013). Differential changes in impulsivity and sensation seeking and the escalation of substance use from adolescence to early adulthood. *Development and Psychopathology*, *25*(1), 223–239. https://doi.org/10.1017/S0954579412000284.

Quiñones-Camacho, L. E., Fishburn, F. A., Camacho, M. C., Wakschlag, L. S., & Perlman, S. B. (2019). Cognitive flexibility-related prefrontal activation in preschoolers: A biological approach to temperamental effortful control. *Developmental Cognitive Neuroscience*, *38*, 100651. https://doi.org/10.1016/j.dcn.2019.100651.

Rabinowitz, J. A., Drabick, D. A., & Reynolds, M. D. (2016). Youth withdrawal moderates the relationships between neighborhood factors and internalizing symptoms in adolescence. *Journal of Youth and Adolescence*, *45*(3), 427–439. https://doi.org/10.1007/s10964-015-0324-y.

Ramer, N. E., Perhamus, G. R., & Colder, C. R. (2024). Reinforcement sensitivity theory and externalizing problems across early adolescence: Testing within-person reciprocal associations. *Developmental Psychology*, *60*(3), 545–559. https://doi.org/10.1037/dev0001689.

Rapee, R. (2014) Preschool environment and temperament as predictors of social and nonsocial anxiety disorder in middle adolescence. *Journal of the American Academy of Child and Adolescent Psychiatry*, *53*, 320–328. https://doi.org/10.1016/j.jaac.2013.11.014.

Rea-Sandin, G., Clifford, S., Doane, L. D., Davis, M. C., Grimm, K. J., Russell, M. T., & Lemery-Chalfant, K. (2023). Genetic and environmental links between executive functioning and effortful control in middle childhood. *Journal of Experimental Psychology: General*, *152*(3), 780–793. https://doi.org/10.1037/xge0001298.

Rhodes, J. D., Colder, C. R., Trucco, E. M., Speidel, C., Hawk, L. W., Jr, Lengua, L. J., ... & Wieczorek, W. (2013). The interaction between self-regulation and motivation prospectively predicting problem behavior in adolescence. *Journal of Clinical Child and Adolescent Psychology*, *42* (5), 681–692. https://doi.org/10.1080/15374416.2013.773515.

Rioux, C., Castellanos-Ryan, N., Parent, S., & Séguin, J. R. (2016). The interaction between temperament and the family environment in adolescent substance use and externalizing behaviors: Support for diathesis-stress or differential susceptibility? *Developmental Review, 40,* 117–150. https://doi .org/10.1016/j.dr.2016.03.003.

Romeo R. D. (2012). The teenage brain: The stress response and the adolescent brain. *Current Directions in Psychological Science, 22*(2), 140–145. https:// doi.org/10.1177/0963721413475445.

Romero, A., & Piña-Watson, B. (2017). Acculturative stress and bicultural stress: Psychological measurement and mental health. In S. J. Schwartz & J. Unger (Eds.), *The Oxford handbook of acculturation and health* (pp. 119–133). New York: Oxford Academic.

Rothbart, M. K. (1986). Longitudinal observation of infant temperament. *Developmental Psychology, 22,* 356–365. https://doi.org/10.1037/0012-1649.22.3.356.

Rothbart, M. K. (1988). Temperament and the development of the inhibited approach. *Child Development, 59,* 1241–1250. www.jstor.org/stable/1130487.

Rothbart, M. K. (2011). *Becoming who we are: Temperament and personality in development.* New York: Guilford Press.

Rothbart, M. K., & Bates, J. E. (1998). Temperament. In W. Damon & N. Eisenberg (Eds.), *Handbook of child psychology: Social, emotional, and personality development,* 5th ed. (pp. 99–166). New York: John Wiley & Sons.

Rothbart, M. K., & Bates, J. E. (2007). Temperament. In W. Damon & N. Eisenberg (Eds.), *Handbook of child psychology: Social, emotional, and personality development* (pp. 105–176). Hoboken, NJ: John Wiley & Sons.

Rothbart, M. K., Ellis, L. K., Rosario Rueda, M., & Posner, M. I. (2003). Developing mechanisms of temperamental effortful control. *Journal of personality, 71*(6), 1113–1144. https://doi.org/10.1111/1467-6494.7106009.

Ruberry, E. J., Lengua, L. J., Crocker, L. H., Bruce, J., Upshaw, M. B., & Sommerville, J. A. (2017). Income, neural executive processes, and preschool children's executive control. *Development and Psychopathology, 29* (1), 143–154. https://doi.org/10.1017/S095457941600002X.

Rubin, K. H., Coplan, R. J., Fox, N. A., & Calkins, S. D. (1995). Emotionality, emotion regulation, and preschoolers' social adaptation. *Development and Psychopathology, 7,* 49–62. https://doi.org/10.1017/S0954579400006337.

Rubin, K. H., Hemphill, S. A., Chen, X., Hastings, P., Sanson, A., Coco, A. L., … & Cui, L. (2006). A cross-cultural study of behavioral inhibition in toddlers: East–West–North–South. *International Journal of Behavioral Development, 30,* 219–226. https://doi.org/10.1177/0165025406066723.

Rubin, K. H., Bowker, J., & Kennedy, A. (2009). Avoiding and withdrawing from the peer group in middle childhood and early adolescence. In K. H. Rubin, W. Bukowski, & B. Laursen (Eds.), *Handbook of peer interactions, relationships, and groups* (pp. 303–321). New York: Guilford Press.

Rudasill, K. M., & Rimm-Kaufman, S. E. (2009). Teacher–child relationship quality: The roles of child temperament and teacher–child interactions. *Early Childhood Research Quarterly, 24*(2), 107–120. https://doi.org/10.1016/j.ecresq.2008.12.003.

Rudasill, K. M., Niehaus, K., Buhs, E., & White, J. M. (2013). Temperament in early childhood and peer interactions in third grade: The role of teacher–child relationships in early elementary grades. *Journal of School Psychology, 51* (6), 701–716. https://doi.org/10.1016/j.jsp.2013.08.002.

Rueda, M. R., Posner, M. I., & Rothbart, M. K. (2004). Attentional control and self-regulation. In R. F. Baumeister & K. D. Vohs (Eds.), *Handbook of self-regulation: Research, theory, and applications, vol. 2,* (pp. 284–299). New York: Guilford Press.

Samek, D. R., Hicks, B. M., Iacono, W. G., McGue, M. (2020). Personality, romantic relationships, and alcohol use disorder symptoms in adolescence and young adulthood: An evaluation of personality × social context interplay. *Development and Psychopathology, 32*(3), 1097–1112. https://doi.org/10.1017/S0954579419001111.

Sánchez-Pérez, N., Fuentes, L. J., Eisenberg, N., & González-Salinas, C. (2018). Effortful control is associated with children's school functioning via learning-related behaviors. *Learning and Individual Differences, 63,* 78–88. https://doi.org/10.1016/j.lindif.2018.02.009.

Sanson, A., Hemphill, S. A., Yagmurlu, B., & McClowry, S. (2011). Temperament and social development. In P. K. Smith & C. H. Hart (eds.), *The Wiley-Blackwell handbook of childhood social development*, 2nd ed. (pp. 227–245). Chichester: Blackwell Publishing.

Santiago, C. D., Etter, E. M., Wadsworth, M. E., & Raviv, T. (2012). Predictors of responses to stress among families coping with poverty-related stress. *Anxiety, Stress & Coping, 25*(3), 239–258. https://doi.org/10.1080/10615806.2011.583347.

Saudino, K. J., & Wang, M. (2012). Quantitative and molecular genetic studies of temperament. In M. Zentner & R. Shiner (Eds.), *Handbook of temperament* (pp. 315–346). New York: Guilford Press.

Scalco, M. D., & Colder, C. R. (2017). Trajectories of marijuana use from late childhood to late adolescence: Can temperament by experience interactions discriminate different trajectories of marijuana use? *Development and*

Psychopathology, 29, 775–790. https://doi.org/10.1017/S09545794 16000468.

Scalco, M. D., Evans, M., & Colder, C. R. (2021). Understanding the progression from early alcohol use experimentation to alcohol use disorder: Testing vulnerability x experience interactions using a two-part latent growth model. *Research on Child and Adolescent Psychopathology, 49*, 789–895. https://doi.org/10.1007/s10802-021-00772-6.

Scaramella, L. V., Sohr-Preston, S. L., Mirabile, S. P., Robison, S. D., & Callahan, K. L. (2008). Parenting and children's distress reactivity during toddlerhood: An examination of direction of effects. *Social Development, 17* (3), 578–595. https://doi.org/10.1111/j.1467-9507.2007.00439.x.

Schmidt, H., Daseking, M., Gawrilow, C., Karbach, J., & Kerner auch Koerner, J. (2022). Self-regulation in preschool: Are executive function and effortful control overlapping constructs? *Developmental Science, 25* (6), e13272. https://doi.org/10.1111/desc.13272.

Schoeps, A., Peterson, E. R., Mia, Y., Waldie, K. E., Underwood, L., D'Souza, S., & Morton, S. M. (2018). Prenatal alcohol consumption and infant and child behavior: Evidence from the growing up in New Zealand cohort. *Early Human Development, 123*, 22–29. https://doi.org/10.1016/j.earlhumdev.2018.06.011.

Schoppe-Sullivan, S. J., Mangelsdorf, S. C., Brown, G. L., & Sokolowski, M. S. (2007). Goodness-of-fit in family context: Infant temperament, marital quality, and early coparenting behavior. *Infant Behavior and Development, 30*(1), 82–96. https://doi.org/10.1016/j.infbeh.2006.11.008.

Schwartz, C. E., Snidman, N., & Kagan, J. (1999). Adolescent social anxiety as an outcome of inhibited temperament in childhood. *Journal of American Academy of Child and Adolescent Psychiatry, 38*, 1008–1015. https://doi.org/10.1097/00004583-199908000-00017.

Schwartz, C. E., Wright, C. I., Shin, L. M., Kagan, J., & Rauch, S. (2003). Inhibited and uninhibited infants "grown up": Adult amygdalar response to novelty. *Science, 300*, 1952–1953. https://doi.org/10.1126/science.1083703.

Schwebel, D. C., & Plumert, J. M. (1999). Longitudinal and concurrent relations among temperament, ability estimation, and injury proneness. *Child Development, 70*(3), 700–712. https://doi.org/10.1111/1467-8624.00050.

Sechi, C., Vismara, L., Rollè, L., Prino, L. E., & Lucarelli, L. (2020). First-time mothers' and fathers' developmental changes in the perception of their daughters' and sons' temperament: Its association with parents' mental health. *Frontiers in Psychology, 11*, 2066. https://doi.org/10.3389/fpsyg.2020.02066.

Shannon, C., Champoux, M., & Suomi, S. J. (1998). Rearing condition and plasma cortisol in rhesus monkey infants. *American Journal of Primatology*, *46*, 311–321. https://doi.org/10.1002/(SICI)1098-2345(1998)46:4<311:: AID-AJP3>3.0.CO;2-L.

Shewark, E. A., Ramos, A. M., Liu, C., Ganiban, J. M., Fosco, G., Shaw, D. S., ... & Neiderhiser, J. M. (2021). The role of child negative emotionality in parenting and child adjustment: Gene–environment interplay. *Journal of Child Psychology and Psychiatry*, *62*(12), 1453–1461. https://doi.org/10.1111/jcpp.13420.

Shimomaeda, L., Thompson, S. F., & Lengua, L. J. (2023). Differential effects of parental control on preschool-age adjustment depending on child effortful control. *Social Development*, *32*(4), 1262–1279. https://doi.org/10.1111/sode.12692.

Shiner, R. L., & Caspi, A. (2012). Temperament and the development of personality traits, adaptations, and narratives. In M. Zentner & R. L. Shiner (Eds.), *Handbook of temperament* (pp. 497–516). New York: Guilford Press. https://doi.org/10.1016/j.earlhumdev.2018.06.011.

Shulman, E. P., Harden, K. P., Chein, J. M., & Steinberg, L. (2015). Sex differences in the developmental trajectories of impulse control and sensation-seeking from early adolescence to early adulthood. *Journal of Youth and Adolescence*, *44*(1), 1–17. https://doi.org/10.1007/s10964-014-0116-9.

Skinner, O. D., & McHale, S. M. (2022). Family gender socialization in childhood and adolescence. In D. P. VanderLaan & W. I. Wong (Eds.), *Gender and sexuality development: Contemporary theory and research* (pp. 233–253). Cham: Springer.

Slagt, M., Dubas, J. S., Deković, M., & van Aken, M. A. (2016). Differences in sensitivity to parenting depending on child temperament: A meta-analysis. *Psychological Bulletin*, *142*(10), 1068–1110. https://doi.org/10.1037/bul0000061.

Snyder, H. R., Gulley, L. D., Bijttebier, P., Hartman, C. A., Oldehinkel, A. J., Mezulis, A., ... & Hankin, B. L. (2015). Adolescent emotionality and effortful control: Core latent constructs and links to psychopathology and functioning. *Journal of Personality and Social Psychology*, *109*(6), 1132–1149. https://doi.org/10.1037/pspp0000047.

Soydan, S. B., & Akalin, N. (2022). The moderating effects of a child's self-regulation skills in the relationship between a child's temperament and the behaviour of the parents. *Early Child Development and Care*, *192*(2), 263–277. https://doi.org/10.1080/03004430.2020.1755666.

Spencer, M. B., Lodato, B. N., Spencer, C., Rich, L., Graziul, C., & English-Clarke, T. (2019). Innovating resilience promotion: Integrating cultural practices, social ecologies and development-sensitive conceptual strategies for advancing child well-being. *Advances in Child Development and Behavior, 57*, 101–148. https://doi.org/10.1016/bs.acdb.2019.05.005.

Spinrad, T. L., Eisenberg, N., & Gaertner, B. M. (2007). Measures of effortful regulation for young children. *Infant Mental Health Journal, 28*, 606–626. https://doi.org/10.1002/imhj.20156.

Spinrad, T. L., Eisenberg, N., Granger, D. A., Eggum, N. D., Sallquist, J., Haugen, R. G., . . . & Hofer, C. (2009). Individual differences in preschoolers' salivary cortisol and alpha-amylase reactivity: Relations to temperament and maladjustment. *Hormones and Behavior, 56*(1), 133–139. https://doi.org/10.1016/j.yhbeh.2009.03.020.

Sportel, B. E., Nauta, M. H., de Hullu, E., de Jong, P. J., & Hartman, C. A. (2011). Behavioral inhibition and attentional control in adolescents: Robust relationships with anxiety and depression. *Journal of Child and Family Studies, 20*(2), 149–156. https://doi.org/10.1007/s10826-010-9435-y.

Spry, E. A., Aarsman, S. R., Youssef, G. J., Patton, G. C., Macdonald, J. A., Sanson, A., . . . & Olsson, C. A. (2020). Maternal and paternal depression and anxiety and offspring infant negative affectivity: A systematic review and meta-analysis. *Developmental Review, 58*, 100934. https://doi.org/10.1016/j.dr.2020.100934.

Steinberg L. (2008). A social neuroscience perspective on adolescent risk-taking. *Developmental Review, 28*(1), 78–106. https://doi.org/10.1016/j.dr.2007.08.002.

Steinberg, L., Albert, D., Cauffman, E., Banich, M., Graham, S., & Woolard, J. (2008). Age differences in sensation seeking and impulsivity as indexed by behavior and self-report: Evidence for a dual systems model. *Developmental Psychology, 44*(6), 1764–1778. https://doi.org/10.1037/a0012955.

Stevens, C., Lauinger, B., & Neville, H. (2009). Differences in the neural mechanisms of selective attention in children from different socioeconomic backgrounds: An event-related brain potential study. *Developmental Science, 12*(4), 634–646. https://doi.org/10.1111/j.1467-7687.2009.00807.x.

Stifter, C. A., & Moding, K. J. (2019). Temperament in obesity-related research: Concepts, challenges, and considerations for future research. *Appetite, 141*, 104308. https://doi.org/10.1016/j.appet.2019.05.039.

Stifter, C. A., Putnam, S., & Jahromi, L. (2008). Exuberant and inhibited toddlers: Stability of temperament and risk for problem behavior. *Development and Psychopathology, 20*(2), 401–421. https://doi.org/10.1017/S0954579408000199.

Stocker, C., Dunn, J., & Plomin, R. (1989). Sibling relationships: Links with child temperament, maternal behavior, and family structure. *Child Development, 60* (3), 715–727. https://www.jstor.org/stable/1130737.

Straight, A. D., Gallagher, K. C., & Kelley, K. (2008). Infant temperament moderates relations between maternal parenting in early childhood and children's adjustment in first grade. *Child Development, 79*, 186–200. https://doi .org/10.1111/j.1467-8624.2007.01119.x.

Strickhouser, J. E., & Sutin, A. R. (2020). Family and neighborhood socioeconomic status and temperament development from childhood to adolescence. *Journal of Personality, 88*(3), 515–529. https://doi.org/10.1111/jopy.12507.

Suárez-Orozco, C., Marks, A. K., Abo-Zena, M. M. (2016). Introduction: Unique and shared experiences of immigrant-origin children and youth. In C. Suárez-Orozco, M. M. Abo-Zena, & A. K. Marks (Eds.), *Transitions: The development of children of immigrants* (pp. 1–26). New York: New York University Press.

Suárez-Orozco, C., Motti-Stefanidi, F., Marks, A., & Katsiaficas, D. (2018). An integrative risk and resilience model for understanding the adaptation of immigrant-origin children and youth. *American Psychologist, 73*(6), 781–796. https://doi.org/10.1037/amp0000265.

Suor, J. H., Sturge-Apple, M. L., Davies, P. T., & Jones-Gordils, H. R. (2019). The interplay between parenting and temperament in associations with children's executive function. *Journal of Family Psychology, 33*(7), 841–850. https://doi.org/10.1037/fam0000558.

Super, C. M., & Harkness, S. (1986). The developmental niche: A conceptualization at the interface of child and culture. *International Journal of Behavioral Development, 9*, 545–569. https://doi.org/10.1177/ 016502548600900409.

Sutton, S. K., & Davidson, R. J. (1997). Prefrontal brain asymmetry: A biological substrate of the behavioral approach and inhibition systems. *Psychological Science, 8*(3), 204–210. https://doi.org/10.1111/j.1467-9280 .1997.tb00413.x.

Tackett, J. L., Krueger, R. F., Iacono, W. G., & McGue, M. (2008). Personality in middle childhood: A hierarchical structure and longitudinal connections with personality in late adolescence. *Journal of Research in Personality, 42*(6), 1456–1462. https://doi.org/10.1016/j.jrp.2008.06.005.

Tandon, P., Thompson, S., Moran, L., & Lengua, L. (2015). Body mass index mediates the effects of low income on preschool children's executive control, with implications for behavior and academics. *Childhood Obesity, 11*(5), 569–576. https://doi.org/10.1089/chi.2014.0071.

Tarullo, A. R., Mliner, S., & Gunnar, M. R. (2011). Inhibition and exuberance in preschool classrooms: Associations with peer social experiences and changes in cortisol across the preschool year. *Developmental Psychology*, *47*(5), 1374–1388. https://doi.org/10.1037/a0024093.

Taylor, Z. E., Eisenberg, N., Spinrad, T. L., & Widaman, K. F. (2013). Longitudinal relations of intrusive parenting and effortful control to ego-resiliency during early childhood. *Child Development*, *84*(4), 1145–1151. https://doi.org/10.1111/cdev.12054.

Thomas, A., & Chess, S. (1977). *Temperament and development*. New York: Brunner/Mazel.

Thompson, S. F., Zalewski, M., & Lengua, L. J. (2014). Appraisal and coping styles account for the effects of temperament on pre-adolescent adjustment. *Australian Journal of Psychology*, *66*(2), 122–129. https://doi.org/10.1111/ajpy.12048.

Thompson, S. F., Zalewski, M., Kiff, C. J., & Lengua, L. J. (2018). A state-trait model of cortisol in early childhood: Contextual and parental predictors of stable and time-varying effects. *Hormones and Behavior*, *98*, 198–209. https://doi.org/10.1016/j.yhbeh.2017.12.009.

Thompson, S. F., Klein, M. R., Ruberry, E. J., Kiff, C. J., Moran, L., Zalewski, M., & Lengua, L. J. (2021). Clarifying the unique effects of pre- and postnatal depression on pre-schoolers' adjustment. *Infant and Child Development*, *30*(1), e2202. https://doi.org/10.1002/icd.2202.

Thompson, S. F., Monini, N., Shimomaeda, L., Green, L., Whiley, D., & Lengua, L. J. (n.d.). New mothers' experiences of childhood adversity and current context of economic adversity predict parent and infant RSA. Unpublished paper.

Thompson, S. F., Shimomaeda, L., Calhoun, R., Metje, A., Nurius, P. S., Whiley, D. J., & Lengua, L. J. (2024). Biological and social cascades of prenatal contextual risk and maternal psychological distress to early-childhood adjustment. *Developmental Psychology*.

Tiego, J., Bellgrove, M. A., Whittle, S., Pantelis, C., & Testa, R. (2020). Common mechanisms of executive attention underlie executive function and effortful control in children. *Developmental Science*, *23*(3), e12918. https://doi.org/10.1111/desc.12918.

Trentacosta, C. J., Hyde, L. W., Shaw, D. S., & Cheong, J. (2009). Adolescent dispositions for antisocial behavior in context: The roles of neighborhood dangerousness and parental knowledge. *Journal of Abnormal Psychology*, *118*, 564–575. https://doi.org/10.1037/a0016394.

Tsai, J. L., & Chentsova-Dutton, Y. (2002). Understanding depression across cultures. In I. H. Gotlib & C. L. Hammen (Eds.), *Handbook of depression* (pp. 467–491). London: Guilford Press.

Tschann, J. M., Kaiser, P., Chesney, M. A., Alkon, A., & Boyce, W. T. (1996). Resilience and vulnerability among preschool children: Family functioning, temperament, and behavior problems. *Journal of the American Academy of Child and Adolescent Psychiatry, 35*(2), 184–192. https://doi.org/10.1097/00004583-199602000-00012.

Turner-Cobb, J. M., Rixon, L., & Jessop, D. S. (2008). A prospective study of diurnal cortisol responses to the social experience of school transition in four-year-old children: Anticipation, exposure, and adaptation. *Developmental Psychology, 50*, 377–389. https://doi.org/10.1002/dev.20298.

Ueno, M., Uchiyama, I., Campos, J. J., Dahl, A., & Anderson, D. I. (2012). The organization of wariness of heights in experienced crawlers. *Infancy: The Official Journal of the International Society on Infant Studies, 17*(4), 376–392. https://doi.org/10.1111/j.1532-7078.2011.00083.x.

Urban Institute (2019, 14 March). Part of us: A data-driven look at children of immigrants. www.urban.org/features/part-us-data-driven-look-children-immigrants.

Valiente, C., Swanson, J., & Lemery-Chalfant, K. (2012). Kindergartners' temperament, classroom engagement, and student–teacher relationship: Moderation by effortful control. *Social Development, 21*(3), 558–576. https://doi.org/10.1111/j.1467-9507.2011.00640.x.

Van Beveren, M. L., Mezulis, A., Wante, L., & Braet, C. (2019). Joint contributions of negative emotionality, positive emotionality, and effortful control on depressive symptoms in youth. *Journal of Clinical Child & Adolescent Psychology, 48* (1), 131–142. https://doi.org/10.1080/15374416.2016.1233499.

Van den Bergh, B. R., van den Heuvel, M. I., Lahti, M., Braeken, M., de Rooij, S. R., Entringer, S., . . . & Schwab, M. (2020). Prenatal developmental origins of behavior and mental health: The influence of maternal stress in pregnancy. *Neuroscience & Biobehavioral Reviews, 117*, 26–64. https://doi.org/10.1016/j.neubiorev.2017.07.003.

van den Boom, D. C. (1989). Neonatal irritability and the development of attachment. In G. A. Kohnstamm, J. E. Bates, & M. K. Rothbart (Eds), *Temperament in childhood* (pp. 299–318). Oxford: John Wiley & Sons.

van den Boom, D. C. (1995). Do first-year intervention effects endure? Follow-up during toddlerhood of a sample of Dutch irritable infants. *Child Development, 66*(6), 1798–1816. https://doi.org/10.1111/j.1467-8624.1995.tb00966.x.

van den Boom, D. C., & Hoeksma, J. B. (1994). The effect of infant irritability on mother–infant interaction: A growth-curve analysis. *Developmental Psychology, 30,* 581–590. https://doi.org/10.1037/0012-1649.30.4.581.

van der Mark, I., Bakermans-Kranenburg, M., & van Ijzendoorn, M. (2002). The role of parenting, attachment, and temperamental fearfulness in the prediction of compliance in toddler girls. *British Journal of Developmental Psychology, 20,* 361–378. https://doi.org/10.1348/02615 1002320620299.

Ventura, J. N., & Stevenson, M. B. (1986). Relations of mothers' and fathers' reports of infant temperament, parents' psychological functioning, and family characteristics. *Merrill-Palmer Quarterly, 32*(3), 275–289. www.jstor .org/stable/23086205.

Wachs, T. D (1992). *The nature of nurture.* Newbury Park, CA: Sage.

Wachs, T. D., Kanashiro, H., & Gurkas, P. (2008). Intra-individual variability in infancy: Structure, stability and nutritional correlates. *Developmental Psychobiology, 50,* 217–231. https://doi.org/10.1002/dev.20284.

Wagner, S. L., Cepeda, I., Krieger, D., Maggi, S., D'Angiulli, A., Weinberg, J., & Grunau, R. E. (2016). Higher cortisol is associated with poorer executive functioning in preschool children: The role of parenting stress, parent coping and quality of daycare. *Child Neuropsychology: A Journal on Normal and Abnormal Development in Childhood And Adolescence, 22*(7), 853–869. https://doi.org/10.1080/09297049.2015 .1080232.

Wass, S. V. (2021). The origins of effortful control: How early development within arousal/regulatory systems influences attentional and affective control. *Developmental Review, 61,* 100978. https://doi.org/10.1016/j .dr.2021.100978.

Watamura, S. E., Donzella, B., Alwin, J., & Gunnar, M. R. (2003). Morning-to-afternoon increases in cortisol concentrations for infants and toddlers at child care: Age differences and behavioral correlates. *Child Development, 74*(4), 1006–1020. https://doi.org/10.1111/1467-8624.00583.

Wong, M. S., Mangelsdorf, S. C., Brown, G. L., Neff, C., & Schoppe-Sullivan, S. J. (2009). Parental beliefs, infant temperament, and marital quality: Associations with infant–mother and infant–father attachment. *Journal of Family Psychology, 23*(6), 828–838. https://doi.org/10.1037/ a0016491.

Worobey, J., Peña, J., Ramos, I., & Espinosa, C. (2014). Infant difficulty and early weight gain: Does fussing promote overeating? *Maternal Child Nutrition, 10* (2), 295–303. https://doi.org/10.1111/j.1740-8709.2012.00410.x.

Xu, Y., & Krieg, A. (2014). Shyness in Asian American children and the relation to temperament, parents' acculturation, and psychosocial functioning. *Infant and Child Development*, *23*(3), 333–342. https://doi.org/10.1002/icd.1860.

Yiu, W. Y. V., Choi, J. H., & Chen, X. (2020). Shyness and adaptation across cultures. In L. A. Schmidt & K. L. Poole (Eds.), *Adaptive shyness* (pp. 201–218). Cham: Springer. https://doi.org/10.1007/978-3-030-38877-5_11.

Youssef, G. J., Whittle, S., Allen, N. B., Lubman, D. I., Simmons, J. G., & Yücel, M. (2016). Cognitive control as a moderator of temperamental motivations toward adolescent risk-taking behavior. *Child Development*, *87*(2), 395–404. https://doi.org/10.1111/cdev.12480.

Zalewski, M., Lengua, L. J., Kiff, C. J., & Fisher, P. A. (2012). Understanding the relation of low income to HPA-axis functioning in preschool children: Cumulative family risk and parenting as pathways to disruptions in cortisol. *Child Psychiatry & Human Development*, *43*, 924–942. https://doi.org/10.1007/s10578-012-0304-3.

Zalewski, M., Lengua, L. J., Thompson, S. F., & Kiff, C. J. (2016). Income, cumulative risk, and longitudinal profiles of hypothalamic–pituitary–adrenal axis activity in preschool-age children. *Development and Psychopathology*, *28*(2), 341–353. https://doi.org/10.1017/S0954579415000474.

Zemp, M., Friedrich, A. S., Schirl, J., Dantchev, S., Voracek, M., & Tran, U. S. (2021). A systematic review and meta-analysis of the associations between interparental and sibling relationships: Positive or negative? *PLOS ONE*, *16*(9), e0257874. https://doi.org/10.1371/journal.pone.0257874.

Zhao, J., Ettekal, I., Nickerson, A. B., Schuetze, P., Shisler, S., Godleski, S., . . . & Eiden, R. D. (2022). Child community violence exposure in an at-risk sample: Developmental trajectories, caregiving risks, and the role of child temperament. *Psychology of Violence*, *12*(6), 382–392. https://doi.org/10.1037/vio0000416.

Zhou, Q., Main, A., & Wang, Y. (2010). The relations of temperamental effortful control and anger/frustration to Chinese children's academic achievement and social adjustment: A longitudinal study. *Journal of Educational Psychology*, *102*(1), 180–196. https://doi.org/10.1037/a0015908.

Zohar, A. H., Zwir, I., Wang, J., Cloninger, C. R., & Anokhin, A. P. (2019). The development of temperament and character during adolescence: The processes and phases of change. *Development and Psychopathology*, *31*(2), 601–617. https://doi.org/10.1017/S0954579418000159.

Zordan, L., Sarlo, M., & Stablum, F. (2008). ERP components activated by the "GO!" and "WITHHOLD!" conflict in the random sustained attention to response task. *Brain and Cognition*, *66*(1), 57–64. https://doi.org/10.1016/j.bandc.2007.05.005.

Zorza, J. P., Marino, J., Lemus, S., & Mesas, A. A. (2013). Academic performance and social competence of adolescents: Predictions based on effortful control and empathy. *Spanish Journal of Psychology*, *16*, 1–12. https://doi.org/10.1017/sjp.2013.87.

Cambridge Elements ≡

Child Development

Marc H. Bornstein

National Institute of Child Health and Human Development, Bethesda
Institute for Fiscal Studies, London
UNICEF, New York City

Marc H. Bornstein is an Affiliate of the *Eunice Kennedy Shriver* National Institute of Child Health and Human Development, an International Research Fellow at the Institute for Fiscal Studies (London), and UNICEF Senior Advisor for Research for ECD Parenting Programmes. Bornstein is President Emeritus of the Society for Research in Child Development, Editor Emeritus of *Child Development*, and founding Editor of *Parenting: Science and Practice*.

About the Series

Child development is a lively and engaging, yet serious and real-world subject of scientific study that encompasses myriad theories, methods, substantive areas, and applied concerns. Cambridge Elements in Child Development addresses many contemporary topics in child development with unique, comprehensive, and state-of-the-art treatments of principal issues, primary currents of thinking, original perspectives, and empirical contributions to understanding early human development.

Cambridge Elements ☰

Child Development

Elements in the Series

A full series listing is available at: www.cambridge.org/EICD

Printed in the United States
by Baker & Taylor Publisher Services